HOW TO PREPARE
FOR THE LAST DAYS

HOW TO PREPARE
FOR THE LAST DAYS

Fulfilling God's Purposes

At the End of the Age

Nelson Walters

with

Bob Brown

Ready for Jesus Publications (Wilmington, NC 2018, 2022)

ISBN: 9798815167872

Contents

Do you want "How to Prepare for the Last Days" to come to your town?

Nelson Walters, Marquis Laughlin, Pastor Jake McCandless

A team of skilled and entertaining presenters from Last Days Overcomers are excited to share the scriptures and message of this book with you in an interactive one-day conference. Get your questions answered in the Q&A sessions and help prepare those in your church for the days preceding the greatest moment in history – the day that Jesus comes back.

Contact us at www.lastdaysovercomer.org to discuss how to schedule a conference in your area.

CHAPTER ONE

What Matters Most

*"What matters most is to **focus** on what matters most."*
~Roy Bennett

The most important day in history will be the day that Jesus comes back. Everything changes. He will resurrect our family and friends from the dead. From that day on, we will live with Him forever and rule and reign with Him in justice and righteousness. He will wipe away war, poverty, and crime, heal the environment, and end Satan's rule.

Given how amazing that day will be, the Apostle Peter told us it should be the focus of our lives – we are to be "*looking for and hastening the coming of the day of God* (2 Pet 3:12)." The Apostle Paul also tells us to be looking forward to that day:

> *Looking for the blessed hope and glorious appearing of our great God and Savior Jesus Christ* (Titus 2:13)

Not only are we to look forward to the return of Jesus, we are to prepare for it as well. Just days prior to His crucifixion, Jesus told His disciples:

> *Therefore, you also be ready, for the Son of Man is coming at an hour you do not expect* (Matt 24:44)

These are very clear commands of scripture: look forward and be ready. However, during most of my lifetime,

1

Christians have ignored them and placed their attention on other things: self-improvement, being relevant to the culture, family life, or politics. While none of these things are wrong in and of themselves, these Christians have elevated lessor things over what's most important. Why?

There are several basic reasons. Many have viewed the return of the Lord as a distant event, likely well beyond their lifetimes. They reasoned that since Jesus hasn't come back for 2000 years, it's entirely possible that His return will be delayed hundreds or even thousands of years into the future. (We address this in Chapters Four and Five)

Also, since Jesus said the timing of His return was unknowable, many Christians have concluded that we shouldn't plan for it in any way. Those who tried to predict this event in the past failed miserably. And current churchgoers don't want to be grouped together with them and be labeled as crazy, "tin hat" fanatics. (We address this in Chapter Four)

A third reason is that the return of Jesus scares the bejeebers out of most people. Does anyone really want to face the end of the world as we know it? Does anyone want to confront the wars, famines, and plagues that are prophesied? No, I don't think so. So, many Christians haven't prepared for Jesus' return simply because doing so stirs up fear of the future. (We address this in Chapter Two)

Therefore, for a combination of reasons, most sitting in the pews on Sundays have ignored scripture's call to look forward to and be ready for the return of the Lord. At least that was the case up until March, 2020.

Then suddenly, like a flurry of punches from Mike Tyson, the world experienced the pandemic, the riots, vaccine mandates, *the* election, the Ukraine crisis, runaway inflation, the energy crisis, mass shootings, and threats of nuclear war - difficult times with the premonition of more on the horizon. These rapid-fire events have made people ask: "Is God trying to tell us something by allowing them? Could the Last Days have already started?" In fact, 77% of evangelicals now believe we are living in the Last Days[1].

Not surprisingly, pastors have been asking themselves the same questions. In a recent *Lifeway* Survey, 9 in 10 pastors stated that they believed some of the current events listed above match those Jesus said would occur shortly before his return to Earth. And in that same survey, 56% of Pastors stated they believe Jesus will return in their lifetimes[2].

Secular leaders like notorious World Economic Forum founder, Klaus Schwab, also wonder if an apocalypse has started, "Famine, floods, pestilence, drought, plague, war, and rumors of war: these are the issues facing the World today.[3]"

It seems churchgoers, pastors, and even non-believers know something about this world has changed. We have entered a period of chaos. So, just like a toothache might remind you that you have skipped a few dental visits, these

---

[1] https://religionnews.com/2013/09/11/shock-poll-startling-numbers-of-americans-believe-world-now-in-the-end-times/
[2] https://news.lifeway.com/2020/04/07/vast-majority-of-pastors-see-signs-of-end-times-in-current-events/
[3] https://www.breitbart.com/politics/2022/05/19/eve-of-destruction-klaus-schwab-pledges-the-world-can-find-salvation-at-davos-2022/

earthshaking events have caused believers to recall that Jesus made a promise to return. Maybe, they reason, it's time to begin to think about that return and prepare for it.

But the problem is that after so many generations of not preparing, Christians are unsure what to do. They realize that getting ready for the day Jesus returns simply requires one be saved. But what about preparing for the days and years prior to that return – what this ministry terms the Last Days?

A few mainstream parachurch organizations like Focus on the Family have scrambled to instruct their followers on how to prepare for the end times. But other than a limited number of ideas on their websites, there hasn't been an organized approach to get us ready for the most important day in history. But churchgoers need answers to their questions:

- Have the Last Days truly begun?
- Can a time of extreme difficulty be our blessed hope?
- What specific things does Jesus want us to do prior to His return?

Trying to wrap your head around similar questions may be what prompted you to purchase this book. But I'm sure you're skeptical. You have likely read "end time" books before that have been no help at all. I promise you; this book is different. As you read on, you'll discover that it is unlike any other Last Days' study. It doesn't take a "your doctrine is wrong, mine is right" point of view. It doesn't contain a single chart of when things are going to happen. It doesn't take a political point of view. So, what does it focus on?

Jesus spent 400% more time instructing us on what we should be *doing* to prepare for his return than he did on the events themselves. This book takes the same approach. It emphasizes application not speculation.

KEY POINT: This book doesn't focus on *when* things will happen, but rather on what to *do* when they happen.

So, whatever camp you fall into: whether you think the Rapture is before the Tribulation or you don't, whether you think the Antichrist is some political figure or you don't, or if you're just confused and seeking answers, I wrote this book for you. It is applicable to everyone.

My heart is that this book helps you prepare for Jesus' glorious return in the way that He desires – in the way He has prescribed in His Word. And I pray that you long for it – that you yearn for it as I do. And then, when we stand before Him on that Day, side-by-side, we both hear the greatest words any Christian can hear, "Well done, good and faithful servant. Enter into the joy of your Master." Because that's what matters most.

CHAPTER TWO

Can the Last Days be a Blessed Hope?

Let's address the elephant in the room right off the bat. The entire concept of the Last Days is scary to most people. I mean, who wants to face persecution, economic distress, and natural disasters? Yet, in the previous chapter, we discussed how the Apostle Paul said the return of Jesus was our blessed hope. Is there a disconnect here? Should we feel guilty of being frightened?

No, not at all. Even the writers of the Bible had similar responses when they considered the Last Days. The Prophet Daniel, after seeing a vision of our future, wrote about his reaction to it: "*And I, Daniel, fainted and was sick for days* (Dan 8:27)." After seeing visions of the future, one of the most faithful men of God who ever lived was sickened by what he saw. So, it's no wonder that the rest of us are a bit shaken by these visions as well. You shouldn't feel guilty about fear. It is a normal human emotion.

However, God has given us resources to deal with the chaos of difficult times. That is why we placed this chapter right up front. So, as you read the rest of this book, you can filter each chapter through the lens of the solutions we discuss here.

But what makes hard times especially difficult and fearful in the 21st Century is that they are unexpected. Back in the days of the apostles, hard times and persecution were part of everyday life. All but one of the apostles were martyred, and the Romans frequently martyred Christians. Jesus said, ""*If the world hates you, you know that it hated Me before it hated you* (John 15:18)"

Surprisingly to those of us living in western nations, however, is that according to Open Doors, much of the world is experiencing similar, extremely difficult times, even in 2022. 312 million Christians - that is 1/7 of all Christians worldwide – experienced an "extreme" level of persecution this year. This is the highest percentage of Christian persecution in history[4] - higher than in the days of the apostles. You may live in an insulted part of the world, but in places like Afghanistan and North Korea, Christians are dying, being tortured or raped, and being displaced from the homes. For them, the hard times are *not* a surprise.

What also makes hard times unexpected is that many Christians had hoped Jesus would return before we had to endure *any* difficulties - that somehow, we'd escape all the challenges that scripture tells us are coming. However, this was wishful thinking. The events of the last two years have proven that dream false. Hard times have started and they threaten to get worse with rumors of nuclear war and economic collapse in the news almost every day.

But, although Jesus didn't rescue us from all hard times, He will rescue His faithful believers before God Himself punishes the doers of evil. Of that rescue, there is no doubt:

---

[4] https://www.opendoorsusa.org/christian-persecution/

> *Wait for His Son from heaven, whom He*
> *raised from the dead, even Jesus who delivers*
> *us from the wrath to come*. (1 Thess 1:10)

Jesus is going to take believers into His presence before He punishes those who refuse to repent of their murders, tortures, rapes, thefts, etc. We call that punishment the Eschatological Wrath of God. So, Christians will avoid some of the hard times the Bible predicts when Jesus rescues them – just not all of it.

In fact, scripture specifically tells us believers will endure hardship before that rescue:

> *Because you have kept My command to*
> *persevere, I also will keep you from the hour*
> *of trial which shall come upon the whole*
> *world, to test those who dwell on the earth.*
> (Rev 3:10)

This "keeping from the hour of trial" is generally thought to be the rescue we just discussed. However, notice this passage is a conditional statement. Jesus is going to rescue only those who have kept His command to persevere. (Elsewhere in scripture, this Greek word translated here as "persevere" is better translated as "patient endurance.") Patient endurance implies long suffering. Absolutely everyone rescued by Jesus at His Coming will have patiently endured for the cause of Christ.

So, no matter what end time theory you believe in, scripture tells us churchgoers are going to suffer through some difficult events before Jesus returns as our blessed hope. And those hard times have begun.

Consequently, we are going to all have to prepare ourselves to endure difficulty. What resources are at our disposal? The Apostle John penned these words in the Book of Revelation's final chapter: "Even so, come, Lord Jesus! (Rev 22:20).". In his visions, John saw horrible events, heartbreaking events in the Last Days. Despite all the carnage that will take place, he reasoned the end result of the Last Days makes the means to get there worth the suffering. He was able to say, "Even so, come, Lord Jesus." Even though there will be hardship, he believed what the Apostle Paul believed, that the return of Jesus was our blessed hope.

KEY POINT: The return of Jesus will be such a blessing that it is worth any amount of distress to achieve it.

Unless Christians believe that too, that the return of the Lord is something to yearn for, they won't be able to overcome fear of the Last Days. Additionally, the rest of this book about how to prepare for them won't make much sense either. We need to know at a gut level that His return _is_ a blessed hope.

What's a blessed hope? It's our journey through life that culminates in this singular day when everything changes. It is our ultimate hope, the ultimate destination of our life's journey, and the ultimate destination of God's prophetic plan for this world as well.

Our world is in a fallen state, it is full of disease, war, human trafficking, murder, starvation, and untold heartache – and these things are only getting worse. No one in their right mind would regard these conditions as a perfect world or even a good one. So, God is going to transform all these things at the return of Jesus. If you are "loving your life" and don't want the world as it is to end, it's because you are living in an insulted corner of this fallen world. The majority of the world is suffering and wants it transformed. Certainly, I do.

KEY POINT: this world right now is not the way that God originally envisioned it to be.

God created Adam and Eve in a perfect garden, but sin drove them out of the garden and transmuted the world into the one we find ourselves in today. However, at the return of Jesus, God is going to return things to that pristine environment of peace and beauty that He originally intended.

And true faith is believing that if God says that suffering is necessary in order to make the transformation happen – if it's part of His plan - then that is what is needed. This is such an important point, let me state it again.

KEY POINT: True faith is trusting what God's Word says about the Last Days – even if it involves suffering.

All of us desire an end to war, human trafficking, etc. It is just that we lack God's perspective of things. We all want these things to be different, but God sees the path the world must take to get there. Unfortunately, that path involves suffering. If this doesn't make sense to you, it doesn't have to! God's ways are higher than ours. But, once we trust His perspective, we can accept that troublesome times are necessary.

As an analogy, our life in this fallen world might be compared to that of a young, inner-city child who has never been outside of the ghetto. The streets around that child are violent, dirty, and full of poverty; but they are the only streets the child has known.

If a ministry provides a van to take that child on a beach vacation, the child might initially resist leaving their familiar environment of bullets and garbage. But, once they get to the beach and discover its safety and beauty, it might be hard to take that child back to the ghetto. It is a matter of perspective. You don't know what you don't know until you know.

We need to acquire that type of big picture perspective as we contemplate the return of our Lord. In order to yearn for the blessed hope, we need to know *why* it's our hope. We need to see "the beach."

The Bible is full of references to our hope being fully realized at the return of Jesus. When we read the word "hope" in the New Testament, it almost always refers to hope in the return of the Lord. Did you know that? We are to hope in *"the resurrection of the dead"* (Acts 23:6), *"the hope of glory"* (Col 1:27), *"the one who will arise to rule over the nations"* (Rom 15:12), *"the presence of our Lord Jesus when he comes"* (1 Thess 2:19), and *"the grace to be brought to you when Jesus Christ is revealed at his coming"* (1 Pet 1:13). This is a lot to hope in, and all of these things happen at Jesus' return.

In fact, Paul had this to say about those who only hope in this life and not in the return of the Lord: *"If only for this life we have hope in Christ, we are of all people most to be pitied"* (1 Cor 15:19). Paul tells us if we are only hoping in this life, we are like that inner-city child who doesn't see the big picture of the beautiful beach that lies ahead.

So, let's look at each aspect of what we are commanded to hope for in order to acquire a big picture perspective. Let's begin with the resurrection of the dead. The Apostle Paul defines this event very clearly:

> *But I do not want you to be ignorant, brethren, concerning those who have fallen asleep … God will bring with Him those who sleep in Jesus … For the Lord Himself will descend from heaven with a shout, with the voice of an archangel, and with the trumpet of God. And the dead in Christ will rise first.* (1 Thess 4:13-16)

All of us have those whom we miss who have passed on. They will be reunited with us on that great day because every believer who has died will be made alive again upon Jesus' return. That's better than any beach vacation.

As an example, on the day my father died, he slipped into a coma. My brother called me and told me to come back to Pennsylvania immediately because Dad wouldn't last long. I asked my brother to put the phone up to Dad's ear. My brother balked, saying, "He's in a coma." I said, "I know, but he'll still hear me." I then told Dad everything a son wants to say at that moment.

Mustering every bit of strength that he still had left, my dad opened his eyes one last time and said his final words to me, "I'll meet you there when you get to heaven." I get to see Dad on that great day – and every day after that. *That* is a blessed hope.

Not only will we see our loved ones resurrected, we may be among those rising on that day. I remember the day I had my open-heart surgery. They told me this particular open-heart procedure was high risk, and that I only had a 90% chance of surviving. I clearly remember praying, "Lord, I will either wake up and continue to serve you, or I'll wake up in your presence. Thank you for dying on the cross for me." *That* is a blessed hope. We can live as if we're immortal, because we are until the Lord calls us home. Paul put it this way:

> *Christ will be magnified in my body, whether*
> *by life or by death. For to me, to live is Christ,*
> *and to die is gain.* (Phil 1:20-21)

The second thing we are to hope for is "glory." What does this mean? It is hope in our future "glorification." Glorification is God's final removal of sin from the life and body of His true believers, those who are saved. On that Day, Jesus is going to transform our mortal bodies into bodies like His that cannot sin.

> *We also eagerly wait for the Savior, the Lord*
> *Jesus Christ, who will transform our lowly*
> *body that it may be conformed to His glorious*
> *body.* (Phil 3:20-21)

Not only does this mean that we will not sin again once we are in these new, "Resurrection Bodies," it also likely means we will have some of the power in that body that Jesus displayed after his resurrection. He passed through solid doors and was able to appear and disappear at will. Will we be like that? I believe so. Plus, these bodies won't age or degrade. *That* is an incredible, supernatural, blessed hope.

The third thing we are commanded to hope for at Jesus' return is His reign over the kingdoms of this world. Greed, injustice, unrighteousness, and selfishness; these are the things that mark the governments of our current world. Fallen, imperfect humans rule them, so this should not be a surprise. But at the return of Jesus, He will sweep these things away. And more than that, He will allow us to rule and reign with Him – to share in His making this world the kind of place we desire it to be:

> *And he who overcomes, and keeps My works*
> *until the end, to him I will give power over the*
> *nations — 'He shall rule them with a rod of*
> *iron; They shall be dashed to pieces like the*
> *potter's vessels* (Rev 2: 26-27)

Imagine a world without its current corruption. *That* is also an amazing, blessed hope.

The fourth thing scripture tells us to hope for is our coming inheritance, a dwelling place in the New Jerusalem, a city of beauty and splendor.

> *And he carried me away in the Spirit to a*
> *great and high mountain, and showed me the*
> *great city, the holy Jerusalem, descending out*
> *of heaven from God, having the glory of God.*
> *Her light was like a most precious stone, like*
> *a jasper stone, clear as crystal. Also she had a*

15

great and high wall with twelve gates, and twelve angels at the gates, and names written on them, which are the names of the twelve tribes of the children of Israel ... The construction of its wall was of jasper; and the city was pure gold, like clear glass. The foundations of the wall of the city were adorned with all kinds of precious stones (Rev 21: 14-19)

Imagine living in a city like that in fellowship with all the saints who ever lived – and with Jesus and the Father. *That* is a blessed hope.

The fifth thing scripture tells us to hope for is the very presence of Jesus. Imagine looking into His eyes and seeing His love for you; love that was willing to go to the cross for you. Imagine His beauty. Imagine the peace of being in his presence "*when He comes, in that Day, to be glorified in His saints and to be admired among all those who believe* (2 Thess 1:10)." *That* is the greatest blessed hope of all; being with Jesus.

The presence of our loved ones and friends – forever, a new, immortal, sin-free body – forever, a King who rules in righteousness and justice – forever, living in a city of incredible beauty – forever, and being in the presence of the Prince of Peace and Love -forever; these things are our blessed hope. It is such good news; it is almost impossible to believe. And once we have this perspective of what is coming, it makes what we will endure prior to that all the more tolerable.

*For I consider that the sufferings of this
present time are not worthy to be compared
with the glory which shall be revealed in us.*
(Rom 8:18)

Paul tells us our suffering is so minor as to not begin to compare to the blessings that are coming. These sufferings are like the ride to a beach vacation. If the "beach" is the return of Jesus, the ride itself is the Last Days, the years prior to His return.

I took several such car rides with my parents when I was younger. I remember asking my parents, "Are we there yet?" The reason I asked that question is because the ride from our house to the beach was a boring, six-hour grind. My Dad's car didn't have air-conditioning in those days, and whatever toy I brought along lost its luster after fifteen minutes - only five hours and forty-five minutes to go!

But our challenging ride to beach was more tolerable knowing where we were going - keeping our eyes on our destination. In the analogy, the destination was the beach. But, in reality, it is our blessed hope that we are heading towards. It is the most amazing and incredible destination anyone could imagine.

Keeping our eyes on Jesus, our hope, as we make progress towards that destination doesn't make it easy to endure difficult times, but it makes the chaos more bearable. Now I don't mean to minimize the losses we may encounter on that journey, but consider how each looks in the light of eternity.

If our loved ones are martyred by persecution, we will see them again on that day. If someone takes our life, we will rise on that day. If someone harms our physical body, we will get a new one on that day. If someone takes over our government, Jesus will rule on that day and we'll rule with Him. If someone takes away your home, you'll get a new one in the New Jerusalem that day. There is noting anyone can take away from you that you won't get back.

But there is one thing no one can take away from you:

> *For I am persuaded that neither death nor life, nor angels nor principalities nor powers, nor things present nor things to come, nor height nor depth, nor any other created thing, shall be able to separate us from the love of God which is in Christ Jesus our Lord.* (Rom 8:38-39)

Nothing can ever separate us from God's love that we carry with us throughout all hard times. Paul said in all these things we are more than conquerors. We win because Jesus wins in the end.

Everything done to harm us is temporary. The blessed hope is eternal. That isn't easy to grasp or implement, but it is that simple.

KEY POINT: We overcome chaos in the Last Days by viewing it in light of our destination – the blessed hope.

Additionally, the closer we get to our destination, the more excited we become. Events like the pandemic and the Ukraine War break our hearts for those who are injured by them, but ultimately, they are signs along the road telling us we are getting closer to the "beach," our blessed hope. We need to consider them in that light.

Now this explanation of the blessed hope has prayerfully presented the Last Days in a new light for you. I'm sure it hasn't answered all your questions. But, by the time you complete this book, hopefully we'll have answered all them for you.

CHAPTER THREE

Are We Ready for Jesus?

I didn't always have this perspective of the Last Days; I ignored them like the majority of Christians for the first half of my Christian life. But then one day, I encountered something in the scriptures that shook me to my soul. Something much more frightening than the events of the Last Days: the concept that the Church wasn't ready for Jesus's return. Think about that for a moment. Not only might churchgoers have to endure some difficult times as we mentioned in the last chapter, but they won't be prepared to do it. This broke my heart as I know it breaks God's heart.

I had been reading the Parable of the Ten Virgins in Matthew 25. In that parable, the main protagonists are virgins waiting for the return of their bridegroom. They are also symbolic of the entire Kingdom of Heaven.

> Then the kingdom of heaven shall be likened
> to ten virgins who took their lamps and went
> out to meet the bridegroom. Now five of
> them were wise, and five were foolish.
> (Matt 25:1-2)

Only churchgoers fit these categories. The virgins Jesus is speaking of are those in the pews (churchgoers) who will see the return of the Lord. Half are wise and half are foolish.

21

You may have noticed I used the term "churchgoer" as opposed to the terms "Christian" or "believer." Why is that? The reason is that Jesus is pretty clear that not everyone who thinks they are a Christian truly is saved or truly is a believer. This will become apparent as you continue to read this book. So "churchgoer" is a term we use throughout this book for all those attending our churches - both the wise virgins and the foolish.

But there was a rude shock in store for me as I continued to read this parable. In Matt 25:5, these words jumped off the page: "*While the bridegroom was delayed, they **all** slumbered and slept.*" Jesus is clearly teaching that right before his return, all the virgins (the whole Church) will be asleep - not just the foolish virgins - but the wise as well.

I like to consider myself as wise and awake in regard to Jesus, maybe you do too; but this verse said something different. It challenged me; it turned my whole thinking upside down. No matter how I looked at it, no matter what commentary I read, no one had a satisfactory answer for what this verse was teaching. Denomination presidents, seminary professors, pastors, everyone in the pews - Jesus is telling us we're all snoozing. So why is the Church asleep and what are the consequences? I had to know the answer.

I realized the implications of being asleep are that all of us are probably missing some critical understanding of the Last Days. No matter how well we think we understand scripture, we should all approach the topic of the Last Days with humility. For instance, Jesus' primary command for those times was to not be deceived, but do we know what kinds of deception are coming? Jesus also told us to watch, but do we know what to watch for? No. Had our churches been prepared for the pandemic, the riots, or the Ukraine War? Again, No. Yet, pestilence, war, and riots are exactly what Jesus said would mark the Last Days. Instead of being ready for them, we were all asleep and caught by surprise.

And as I continued to read this parable, I discovered an even more unsettling revelation. Jesus taught that only the wise virgins who were ready would go in with Him to the wedding banquet – into heaven.

> The bridegroom came, and those who were
> **ready** went in with him to the wedding; and
> the door was shut. Afterward the other
> virgins came also, saying, 'Lord, Lord, open to
> us!' But he answered and said, 'Assuredly, I
> say to you, I do not know you.'
> (Matt 25:10-12)

Jesus shuts the door of heaven on those who aren't ready - the other 50% waiting for His return. Can being ready for Jesus' return be *that* serious? Can preparation for the Last Days be a salvation issue? Obviously, it can - Jesus told us so. This led me to a jarring conclusion:

KEY POINT: *if Jesus came back today, our churches would not be ready.*

I appreciate that this is a very scandalous statement. If our churches aren't ready for Jesus, we have a problem on our hands. I had always just assumed I was prepared, but in this parable, Jesus is telling us that we aren't as ready as we thought. Only 50% of those who think they are Christians are truly saved. The foolish virgins were waiting for the bridegroom – they thought they were saved - but they weren't. This is a sobering statistic.

And as we saw previously, the wise virgins were asleep as well as the foolish. Most of us weren't ready for the initial events of the Last Days like the pandemic. Most weren't ready for the lock-down of our church buildings, government-imposed vaccine mandates, and most importantly of all, few were prepared to overcome fear by caring for the sick and dying – by expressing the love of Christ in the midst of crisis. We missed these things because we didn't know where we were in God's timeline (in the Last Days), and we didn't know the appropriate actions to take when events began to happen.

In 2022, our ministry conducted a survey of 4500 respondents to determine the attitude Christians had about "sleepiness." A vast majority of the Christians polled, 75%, thought their own church or most churches were asleep in regard to the return of Jesus. And over a third of all respondents no longer attend church for this reason. Over 1500 respondents have left their churches because they aren't being taught about the Last Days.

Therefore, one thing is clear, our churches are asleep just as Jesus told us. We're asleep to the vast mission field that presents itself each Sunday in our pews. And we are asleep as to what God expects us to do during the ever-worsening-events that He will allow on this planet.

KEY POINT: The Last Days are potentially the greatest time of revival and awakening the world has seen – but only if we wake up.

Now, there was a time when Christians weren't asleep. Back in the days of the apostles, they eagerly awaited the return of our Lord – taught about the return of our Lord – and prayed about it. It was the main focus of their worship and faith. But as the years slipped into centuries, the expectation wore off, and the snoring began. Now most Christians don't routinely even think about Jesus' return.

But if you read the Bible carefully, that's not what God intended. Verses about Jesus' glorious return and the years immediately preceding it comprise nearly 25% of the Bible. And in Jesus' last week of life, knowing He was about to die, He shared what He thought were the most important aspects of His message. That week, in His sermon known as the Olivet Discourse, He outlined the events of the Last Days and instructed His followers how to react to and overcome them. The Last Days were at the _core_ of His message. So how can we make them the core of our faith once again? Maybe a few analogies might help.

For believers, the Last Days will be like the end of an American football game. During the two-minute-warning, strategies that the teams employed during the rest of the game are usually discarded in a last-ditch attempt to win. Offenses pass more often, and defenses fall back in a "prevent defense." The Last Days are like that. We need to employ new strategies appropriate with the time that we're living in. The "old wine" (strategies) we had been employing will no longer work in the "new wineskins" of the Last Days. Make no mistake, God expects us to be doing something _different_ right now to get ready for the challenges ahead. That's why He gave us so many commands specific to those days. He expects us to shift strategies and move in a new direction. Life is no longer business-as-usual.

It wasn't business as usual on September 11, 2001 (9/11) either. Some of those on the 78th Floor of the World Trade Center's South Tower were faced with a similar conundrum. The 78th Floor was an inflection point in the Trade Center's elevator system. It was the floor where everyone exited the elevator they had been on and took another elevator to either go up or down.

Fifteen minutes earlier, a plane had hit the North Tower causing a roaring fire. Survivors on the 78th Floor remember looking out the window at the burning inferno. Some said the heat from the fire next door was like "putting your head in an oven." Everyone had to make a decision - whether to continue to go up the elevator or go back down and escape.

Despite the obvious conclusion that everything was not "business-as-usual," an intercom announcement proclaimed the South Tower was secured and workers could return to their floors to work. This is human nature. It is normal to think that nothing out of the ordinary is happening. Some of those on the 78th Floor trusted this announcement and went higher into the Tower - they did not survive. Others trusted their own instinct and left the building. Moments later a second plane struck the South Tower right above the 78th Floor.

You and I are at a similar inflection point in history. Our instincts (or the Holy Spirit) should be telling us that the condition of our world is not business-as-usual and that "normal" isn't coming back. But millions of churchgoers will ignore the warnings God is sending and not take evasive action. They will continue their lives as if nothing unusual has happened or is about to happen in the near future.

In another analogy, the Last Days will be like the end of a college semester when students have put off preparing, and at the last moment, try to "cram" for their final exams. The Last Days are a "final exam," and Christians should be praying and preparing harder than ever as the end draws near.

In the Parable of the Ten Virgins, the five wise virgins had prepared, but the five foolish ones had not. When the virgins are warned that their bridegroom is coming, to their horror, the foolish virgins discover that their lamps are burning out. But it's too late; they don't have time to buy more oil.

> *Then all those virgins arose and trimmed their lamps. And the foolish said to the wise, 'Give us some of your oil, for our lamps are going out.' But the wise answered, saying, 'No, lest there should not be enough for us and you; but go rather to those who sell, and buy for yourselves.' And while they went to buy, the bridegroom came, and those who were ready went in with him to the wedding; and the door was shut.* (Matt 25:7-10)

In the Last Days, it will be too late for many sleepy churchgoers to prepare. They'll realize that they should have been praying, preparing, and studying all along. Part of

27

our preparing for those days is conveying a sense of urgency to all those we come in contact with. Time is short.

Our final analogy of the Last Days is that it's like a hurricane. During the week prior to landfall, those of us who live in the path of the storm take special precautions. When we see the storm coming, the wise among us gas up our trucks and board up our windows. Preparing for the Last Days requires special preparation as well – spiritual, physical, and emotional preparation. We will discuss all three types of preparation in this book.

A hurricane is a very adept metaphor for the Last Days. At the center of a hurricane is what is known as the *eye of the storm*. It is the most intense portion of a cyclone. But prior to the eye hitting land, the outer bands of the hurricane strike. Even though the wind speeds in these outer bands are not as severe, they can still pack a punch.

Figure 1: Outer bands of Hurricane Florence, 2018

In the Last Days, the most severe portion of the storm, the eye of the storm, is known as the Great Tribulation:

> *For then there will be great tribulation, such as has not been since the beginning of the world until this time, no, nor ever shall be.* (Matt 24:21)

Jesus is clear it will be the greatest time of trouble since the world began; worse than the Holocaust and World War II. We do not believe we are in that time just yet; believers may not enter that time at all, but we do believe that the outer bands of the spiritual storm that precede the eye are beginning to make landfall.

In Matt 24:4-8, Jesus called these outer bands of the storm the Beginning of the Birth Pangs. It is this period, or at least the shadows of this period, that 9 out of 10 Pastors think we may be entering as we discussed in Chapter One. We still don't know how far away the eye of the storm is; but the appearance of the initial outer bands tells us it's coming relatively soon.

But focusing on the eye of the storm or even the outer bands is not the proper way to prepare. We need to focus on the return of Jesus! There may be hardships to endure and overcome prior to His return on the clouds, but they will pale in comparison to that glorious day. The spiritual hurricane that is coming shouldn't be our focus, it's only a tool that the Lord will use to help bring about His victory - and to make our work for Him more effective.

In the same way, a natural hurricane can bring Jesus' Kingdom near to those who are distressed. In 2018, Hurricane Florence hit my home town of Wilmington, North Carolina with devastating impact. My church partnered with Convoy of Hope and Samaritan's Purse to send teams into the flooded homes and tree-strewn yards.

I remember working alongside homeowners, rebuilding houses and hope. Hardship sometimes opens the door for the love of Christ to pour in. This is a model of what the Lord has planned for the devastation of the Last Days. We'll discuss how He plans to do this in Chapter Seven.

In summary, why should we prepare for the Last Days? Primarily, because Jesus told us it is a salvation issue! Churchgoers are at risk of having the door of heaven closed on them. And second, based on how our churches reacted during the events of the past few years, we can see even the wise virgins are mostly clueless about what God said is coming and what He wants us doing in the Last Days.

Consequently, this book will systematically walk you through what God has planned for the Last Days, why He is allowing them, and what He plans to accomplish. If we understand God's purposes, we can align ourselves with them.

We will also discuss topics that most Last Days books avoid like the role fear plays, how to deal with the plethora of conflicting Last Days' theories, Satan's plans for the Last Days, and specifics about overcoming deception, violence, economic collapse, and persecution.

But, before we examine what we should be doing in the Last Days, we need to carefully consider why 9 out of 10 Pastors are now convinced that we are entering the early stages of those days. As we discussed in Chapter One, a lot of folks think the return of Jesus is far off. We realize you may agree and think that there is no evidence at all that Jesus is coming soon. You might conclude that if we haven't entered that time of difficulty, then there is no purpose in learning how to prepare for it. You may consider it just wasted effort at best, and potentially harmful at worst.

If you believe this, you may be surprised to discover that the Bible provides us with evidence so we can know if we're that Final Generation before His return. And given the consequences of being wrong, there are few things in life that are more important. A spiritual nap takes quite a rousing for us to wake up, but once we're sure we are the generation who will see Jesus coming – from that moment on, for the rest of our lives - we're wide awake.

CHAPTER FOUR

Are We the Final Generation?

Are we the Final Generation; the one that sees Jesus coming on the clouds? Prior to 2020, many churches didn't think Jesus was coming back anytime soon. However, if they are mistaken and Jesus returns before the Final Generation is warned, the consequences are eternal. Millions of lives and souls may be needlessly lost. And God has told us that He plans to hold those in authority *personally* responsible for not preparing His people should that happen:

> *But if the watchman sees the sword coming*
> *and does not blow the trumpet, and the*
> *people are not warned, and the sword comes*
> *and takes any person from among them, he is*
> *taken away in his iniquity;* ***but his blood I will***
> ***require at the watchman's hand*** (Ezek 33:6)

At first, this may seem incredibly harsh, but hundreds of millions of souls are at stake. God has entrusted the scriptures to the leaders of His Church and set them as "watchmen on the walls." People like me, and possibly you, are to keep watch for the signs of His coming and then blow the trumpet of warning once they see those signs begin to take place. This book is just such a trumpet call.

To which some may say, "Hey, wait a minute. No one knows that day or hour. You can't know the time of Jesus' return with any degree of certainty. Jesus might come in a hundred or even a thousand years. The books I read say there are no signs before His return."

Jesus' return *will* surprise the world, of that there is no doubt. But the assumption that there are no signs isn't accurate. We can't know the exact day or hour of His return, but we can know if we are part of the generation who will see Him coming. The Apostle Paul confirmed this:

> *For you yourselves know perfectly that the day of the Lord so comes as a thief in the night ... But you, brethren, are not in darkness, so that this Day should overtake you as a thief ... therefore let us not sleep, as others do, but let us watch and be sober* (1 Thess 5:2-6)

Paul instructs us that true believers won't know the exact day of Jesus' return; He comes as a thief. But they won't be surprised by the season of His return because they'll be watching. Watching for what? The signs of His coming.

The disciples asked Jesus about these signs just days before He was betrayed and crucified. They wanted to know what we want to know: "How can Christians tell if they are living in the Final Generation?" And Jesus clearly answered that question by means of the Fig Tree Parable, a parable that includes both the phrase: "(the) day and hour no man knows" *and* the signs of his coming. It was a complete answer. To focus on one part of the answer without the other is to misunderstand what Jesus was trying to say.

He began this teaching, "Now learn this parable from the fig tree." Jesus thought this teaching was so important that He commanded his followers to *learn* this parable and what its interpretation meant. It was the only time in scripture that He gave His followers that command.

Learning this parable is probably a great place for any Christian to start understanding the Last Days. From it, you can figure out if you are part of the Final Generation; and therefore, if you need to begin to prepare for those times.

> *Now learn this parable from the fig tree:*
> *When its branch has already become tender*
> *and puts forth leaves, you know that summer*
> *is near. So you also, when you see all these*
> *things, know that it is near—at the doors!*
> *Assuredly, I say to you, this generation will by*
> *no means pass away till all these things take*
> *place. Heaven and earth will pass away, but*
> *My words will by no means pass away. But of*
> *that day and hour no one knows, not even*
> *the angels of heaven, but My Father only.*
> (Matt 24:32-36)

The parable explains what Christians can know about Jesus's return and what they can't. In terms of what we can know, Jesus told us that when something known as the "fig tree" sprouts leaves, we can know that "summer" is near. And, when Christians see all the things that He spoke of previously in Matthew 24 happening at the same time (deception, war, famine, etc.), then they can know that the end of the age is very near - right at the door. Those are the two things that Christians can know. Christians can't know the exact day or hour of Jesus' return, but believers *can* know if they are part of the generation that will see Him coming. The identity of the "fig tree" tells us that.

What is the "fig tree?" The meaning of the parable hinges on its identity. Is it a symbol, or is it just an analogy? The answer makes an enormous difference. If it a symbol, if the fig tree represents something specific, when we see that "something specific" sprouting leaves, we'll know that the Final Generation has begun.

However, if it's just an analogy; if Jesus was saying it was just any old tree that sprouts leaves, then it will give us no real information. To decide which it is, we need to let scripture-interpret-scripture. The Prophet Hosea is the first to tell us:

> I found **Israel** Like grapes in the wilderness; I saw your fathers as the firstfruits on the **fig tree** in its first season (Hos 9:10)

Hosea tells us the fig tree is the nation of Israel, but is there a second witness? Jeremiah the Prophet says:

> Thus says the Lord, the God of Israel: 'Like these good **figs**, so will I acknowledge those who are carried away captive from **Judah**"
> (Jer 24:5)

Judah is part of the nation of Israel, and they are equated with figs. Is there even a third witness? There is, and it happens to the Lord Jesus, Himself. In fact, Jesus used this symbol for Israel three times in His ministry.

First. He told the Parable of the Barren Fig Tree in Luke 13: 6-9. It's about a tree that had no fruit in the first three years

He visited it. This would equate to the first three years of Jesus' ministry. So again, the fig tree is a symbol of the nation of Israel, based in Jerusalem, which Jesus visited yearly.

Then in Mark 11: 12-20, Jesus cursed a fig tree for not bearing fruit, and it withered and miraculously died overnight. In the morning, the disciples saw this withered tree. That was the **very same day** Jesus would tell them the Fig Tree Parable. So, when Jesus said, "learn the parable from the fig tree," this miraculous withered tree was prominent in their minds. These aren't two unrelated accounts – it was the same day.

And just **hours** before telling the parable, Jesus had also confronted the Jewish leaders in the temple saying:

> *Your house is left to you desolate; for I say to you, you shall see Me no more till you say, 'Blessed is He who comes in the name of the Lord!'* (Matt 23:38)

That was the moment Jesus withered the nation of Israel just as he withered the Fig Tree! This confrontation was also fresh in the disciples' minds; and in fact, that heated denunciation of Israel by Jesus was the very reason that the disciples had begun to ask Him about the Last Days and the signs of His coming.

Therefore, the Fig Tree Parable is about this withered fig tree they had seen earlier that morning. It can't be about anything else. And the fig tree, according to scripture, is a symbol for the nation of Israel.

Israel was the withering fig tree; but in the Fig Tree Parable, Jesus described the tree as coming back to life - as putting forth new leaves in the spring. When did this happen? In the spring, on May 14, 1948 when Israel was reborn as a nation in one day. That marked the beginning of the Final Generation. The fig tree sprouting leaves is the first sign of Jesus' Second Coming.

Those of us born after 1948 don't quite realize how incredible the rebirth of Israel was. There are no longer ancient Assyrians, Jebusites, or Amalekites; but Israel exists again. What a miracle! And the generation who saw Israel become a nation in 1948 is still alive. For instance, Billy Graham's daughter, evangelist Anne Graham Lotz, was born that year.

The creation of the state of Israel marks the beginning of the Final Generation; and this makes sense as there are a multitude of end time passages that require Israel to exist in the Last Days. Numerous passages in the prophets like Isaiah, Jeremiah, Joel, Ezekiel, Zechariah, as well as in the Gospels all refer to a Last Days Israel. That's why, in our opinion, Israel becoming a nation in 1948 is the fig tree sprouting leaves, the fig tree coming back to life.

But what about the term "summer?" Jesus said when the fig tree sprouted leaves, we could know "summer" was near. What did He mean by that? Is that a symbol as well? Yes, it is; although a gentile Christian believer likely won't recognize it. However, a messianic believer might.

In the Hebraic calendar, there is a 3-week period (17th of Tammuz till the 9th of Av) during summer which is observed as a period of mourning. It was during this period that both Holy Temples were destroyed (in 586 BC and AD 70). It is the bleakest period of the Jewish year. It is a time of fasting, no weddings are performed, and even haircuts are not permitted. This reference would not have been lost on the disciples who would have recognized it as a symbol for the time of extreme difficulties – the Last Days. This is *especially* true because the disciples were asking about the coming destruction of the temple which happened during this period in the summer.

An Israeli Pastor, Howard Bass, also explained to me that "summer" is used in this verse as a Hebraic wordplay. The last part of the Hebrew word "summer" (Kay-itz) sounds like the Hebrew word for "end." (qets). So, when Jesus said, "You know that summer is near," it sounded like, "you know the end is near" to his disciples.

KEY POINT: *Summer is a symbol for the Last Days.*

Therefore, the first thing that Jesus told us believers could know was that after the rebirth of the nation of Israel, the time of extreme difficulty would not be far behind. Summer would be near. He also said that the generation who sees the fig tree put forth leaves would also see all the things in Matt 24 take place – this includes the return of Jesus on the clouds (Matt 24:30).

This is incredibly important because the rebirth of Israel isn't some long ago biblical event. Jesus was speaking of the days we are living in right now. He told the disciples that He would return to the generation that saw the rebirth of the fig tree – the nation of Israel. That generation would live to see three things: the rebirth of Israel, the times of extreme difficulty, and then His glorious return on the clouds.

The Last Days
Signs in Matt 24

Figure 2: The Final Generation

There are probably those who will say, "Couldn't the generation of the Fig Tree Parable refer to the generation alive at the time of Jesus?" After all, the parable states:

> So you also, when you see all these things,
> know that it is near—at the doors! Assuredly,
> I say to you, **this generation** will by no means
> pass away till all these things take place.
> (Matt 24:33-34)

To a First Century Israelite, the term "this generation" could mean either the generation alive at that time or it could mean a different generation. That's unlike modern English where it primarily means the current generation. However, before we get into that, look at what would be necessary for it to be a First Century generation. All the things in Matt 24 would have had to have already taken place:

- The Gospel would be preached to all the ethnic groups in the whole world (Matt 24:14) – that still hasn't happened,
- A great tribulation would occur in the whole world (Matt 24:21) – that still hasn't happened,
- A false messiah would perform miracles so convincing they might even deceive the elect (Matt 24:24) – that still hasn't happened,
- Jesus would appear in the sky and His angels would gather His elect from the entire earth (Matt 24:31) – that still hasn't happened.

So obviously, when Jesus used the term: *this generation*, He meant a different generation than the one alive at that time. What generation is that?

The Greek word we translate as "this" could also refer to the last of something mentioned; not just the generation living at that time, but to the last generation Jesus mentioned. That generation was the one that would see the fig tree come back to life. So in this parable, the term "this generation" meant the generation who saw the fig tree put forth leaves in 1948, and who will also see all the things that Jesus revealed in Matt 24.

KEY POINT: *We are the Final Generation.*

But how long is a generation? If we know, it seems from this parable that we can date set the return of Jesus. But, we can't. Remember we can't know the day or the hour.

However, The Psalm of Moses gives us one estimate:

> The days of our lives are **seventy years**; and if by reason of strength, they are **eighty years** (Psalm 90:10)

Genesis gives us the upper limit of what a generation is:

> And the Lord said, "My Spirit shall not strive with man forever, for he is indeed flesh; yet his days shall be **one hundred and twenty years**." (Gen 6:3)

Humans don't live longer than 120 years. If the upper limit of man's life is 120 years, it sets an upper limit of what a generation is. If this thinking is correct, that limit for the return of Jesus would be the year 2068 (1948 plus 120 years). It is not assured, but incredibly likely that somewhere between now and then, Jesus is coming back. If you remember, nearly 60% of Pastors now believe He is coming back in their lifetime.

Did you know that ten-year-olds in 2022 will only be 56 that year, 2068? They need to know this information. Everyone does.

And if God's definition of a generation is the one given in the Psalm of Moses, 80 years, that would mean Jesus will return in less than six years – before the end of 2028!! (1948 plus 80 years). We can't rule that possibility out.

As we said, everyone in the pews needs to hear this. It will change the way they live, because if we can prove to them that they are that generation, it creates fearlessness, a sense of overcoming, and a sense of destiny.

Want to get your congregation excited about Jesus? Want to help them overcome their sin? Then help them prove to themselves they are the Final Generation and they will live like it. If they know that Jesus is coming in the very near future, most likely in their own lifetimes or the lifetime of their children, then the things of this world will grow dimly pale in comparison. And the focus of your family and church will be on the great commission, not on money or politics.

However, perhaps you aren't completely convinced by the Fig Tree Parable and need more evidence that we are the Final Generation. Can we say with assurance that we differ from all previous generations that mistakenly said that Jesus was coming in their lifetimes? That is exactly what we plan to demonstrate in the next chapter as we provide eight more proofs that we are the Final Generation.

CHAPTER FIVE

Eight More Proofs

In the last chapter, we provided biblical evidence that we are the Final Generation before the return of Jesus by means of the Fig Tree Parable. This was *the* teaching that Jesus used to answer the disciples' question of when the Last Days would take place. But this is far from the only proof.

The other eight proofs in this chapter involve the spiritual discipline of "watching" or being "watchful." In the New Testament, Jesus, Paul, Peter, and John all refer to this discipline. In fact, they refer to it 23 times! It is a key way we prepare for the Last Days – by watching.

God not only wants us to learn how to "watch" so that we can be aware of what "time it is" – where we are on God's timetable - but also as an evangelistic endeavor. Evangelistic? Yes! Fulfilled prophecy is the greatest proof we have that Jesus is who He says He is, and that He is going to do what He said He would do. Fulfilled prophecy proves the credibility of God and the Bible.

In the second chapter of the Book of Acts, in Peter's first sermon, he used fulfilled prophecy to lead 3000 souls to faith in Jesus on that Pentecost day. We will have that same opportunity in the Last Days - if we learn how to "watch."

The Greek word translated "watch" carries the meaning of being alert and staying awake. This term was used in biblical

45

times in regard to a night watchman who would be stationed on the wall of a fort or city. He was to keep alert for enemy activity during one of the aptly named "four watches of the night." It was important that the watchman stay awake and not fall asleep. If you remember in the last chapter, we saw how God will hold the watchman accountable for those who are lost by his negligence. Jesus referred to this concept of watching directly and associated it with His return:

> Watch therefore, for you do not know when the master of the house is coming—in the evening, at midnight, at the crowing of the rooster, or in the morning— lest, coming suddenly, he find you sleeping. And what I say to you, I say to all: Watch!" (Mark 13:35-37)

Did you notice that Jesus referred to all four watches: evening, midnight, the crowing of the rooster, and morning? And He requires all of us to stay awake and alert at all times during our watch. In the Book of Revelation, He indicates this in one of the strangest passages in the Bible:

> Behold, I am coming as a thief. Blessed is he who watches, and keeps his garments, lest he walk naked and they see his shame (Rev 16:15)

Again, this passage is linked to Jesus coming on the clouds like a thief. But what is this about losing your garments and going naked? Like we said, this is a most bizarre passage. However, the 19th Century Jewish convert to Christianity,

Alfred Edersheim, relates how a curious Jewish tradition is related to watching in his book, "The Temple."

> "During the night the captain of the Temple made his rounds. On his approach the guards had to rise and salute him in a particular manner. Any guard found asleep when on duty was beaten, or his garments were set on fire. The confession of one of the Rabbis is on record that, on a certain occasion, his own maternal uncle had actually undergone the punishment of having his clothes set on fire by the captain of the Temple" (Edersheim, "The Temple").[5]

Therefore, the picture that Jesus paints in this odd passage from Revelation is that of a sleeping watchman having his clothes set on fire because he fell asleep. And upon waking and finding himself engulfed in flames, the watchman rips off his clothes and runs out of the Temple in shame. Not a lesson one would soon forget. So, watchfulness is associated with not falling asleep.

And falling asleep is exactly what Jesus accused all of us of in the Parable of the Ten Virgins. Personally, I was not interested in having my clothes set on fire, so I continued my journey to figure out what watchfulness entailed.

> KEY POINT: *We are all commanded to be watchful for Jesus' return and not to fall asleep on our watch.*

---

[5] https://biblehub.com/commentaries/revelation/16-15.htm

In these last two passages and dozens more, we see that watchfulness is a key ingredient in our preparation for the Last Days. But how does one do that? We know that Jesus is going to appear suddenly on a day and hour that no man knows. Obviously, we aren't going to stand around with our eyes on the sky. It's not that kind of watching.

Rather it is watching for the events that the Bible indicates will happen prior to the return of Jesus. When we see these things beginning to take place, we know the time is near.

And this explains why the Church is now "asleep." If we aren't thinking about Jesus' return on a regular basis, then we won't notice events in our world that could indicate the end is approaching. This is such an important point, let me repeat it:

KEY POINT: *If you are not anticipating Jesus returning soon, you will miss the signs of His coming. You will be "asleep."*

It is our opinion that this is exactly what Jesus meant in the Parable of the Ten Virgins when He said they all "slumbered and slept." Jesus was saying the entire Church will be unaware they are the Final Generation (they're "asleep") and will miss the signs of His coming. And there is enormous risk in being asleep.

When the foolish virgins are finally awakened, it is too late for them to prepare. Jesus locks the door of heaven before they can enter. That is Jesus' main point in the parable: sleeping churchgoers will only recognize the return of Jesus is upon them when it is too late to prepare. This is a serious problem. We need to awaken them to begin watching.

Now that we finally understand the symbolism of Jesus' words in Matt 25, let me give you an example of how this discipline of watching works.

Would you agree that once the Great Tribulation starts, those alive at the time are the Final Generation? Of course! Because Jesus returns just 3 1/2 years later. So everyone alive at that time is part of the Final Generation. So if we see signs that the Great Tribulation is approaching, we can infer that we too are part of the Final Generation.

In Matt 24, Jesus told us when the Great Tribulation begins. He was very specific that a horrible abomination would take place on the holy place in Jerusalem (Matt 24:15), and that this abomination was described by the prophet Daniel.

In three separate chapters of his book, Daniel gives us the events of the abomination. He tells us that the abomination begins when the daily, regular sacrifice of lambs on the temple mount is stopped. When the sacrifice is ended, then the abomination will happen, and the Great Tribulation will begin. But there is a problem. Those sacrifices haven't taken place for 1900 years! So logically, they can't end until they begin again. Therefore, the big question is: are we getting close to them starting?

Within the last 10 years, the Temple Institute, an organization in Jerusalem, has built a mobile altar that can be rolled into place on the Temple Mount, they've constructed all the necessary Temple implements, and have trained priests to perform these sacrifices. All that is needed for the sacrifices to start again is a decision from the Prime

Minister of Israel to go forward with the sacrifices. We are that close to seeing this incredible Last Days sign.

This is an example of how to be watchful. Noticing something in world events that is directly tied to the return of Jesus. In this case, it is noticing the activities in Israel related to the potential re-starting of animal sacrifices. Only those who are awake will notice this type of news story.

Also please observe that only our generation, the Final Generation, could be aware that these things were happening in Israel. The media culture and network of cell phones we almost all carry allows us to "watch" as these events happen half way around the world. But although Jesus has given us the technology to "see" these events happening, how many churchgoers are awake and aware of this Last Days sign?

Unfortunately, the Church is asleep just as Jesus said. However, you and I have the opportunity to help wake them up. That is part of what Jesus expects of us.

And if you haven't realized it yet, the birth of the nation of Israel is another example of watchfulness. Bible scholars at the time (1948) realized that Israel existing as a nation was an important prerequisite for the Last Days. And they understood that this event marked the beginning of a Last Days clock ticking down.

Some scholars even rightly concluded that the birth of the nation of Israel was tied to The Fig Tree Parable. Unfortunately, the most infamous is Edgar Whisenant, who wrote *"88 Reasons Why the Rapture Will be in 1988"* – obviously he was mistaken. His mistake was trying to date set the return of Jesus rather than simply acknowledging that we were now in the Final Generation, the generation that sees the fig tree spouting leaves. He tried to be too specific in what we could know.

This one misguided book has done more harm to the biblical discipline of watchfulness than all the positive combined. Rather than making the birth of the nation of Israel a landmark in the Christian Church, this book burned a lot of pastors who got caught up in Whisenant's hysteria. This caused them to totally abandon the idea of watchfulness.

Very few conservative churches now regularly update their flock on potentially prophetic events out of fear of getting "burned" again. But this fear is unfounded as long as we don't make Whisenant's mistake - don't use these signs to date set the return of the Lord. These events are meant to guide us into knowledge of the season we are in (something we can know), not to give us specific dates.

So let's look at some additional signs that we are the Final Generation. The second sign is that in the Last Days, Jerusalem will become a "cup of drunkenness for the nations all around" (Zech 12:2). This is exactly what we see in the Middle East. Israel and Jerusalem are opposed by many of their Muslim neighbors. This was not true until 1948 when Israel became a nation again and the fig tree put forth leaves.

Additionally, specific prophecies like Ezekiel 38 give details about who these enemies are. And these prophecies are beginning to be fleshed out. For instance, Turkey is now quietly assembling a coalition of nations that exactly matches the famous Gog of Magog alliance found in that passage in Ezekiel 38. Never before in history has an alliance with these precise nations existed in opposition to Israel, but it is forming right now.

And SHOCKINGLY, the establishing of this alliance is also part of the Fig Tree Parable! In Luke's version of this parable, we read something slightly different than Matthew's version that we studied in the last chapter; and that portion may be speaking of these same Muslim nations.

> *Look at the fig tree, and all the trees. When*
> *they are already budding, you see and know*
> *for yourselves that summer is now near* (Luke
> 21:29-30)

In this version from the Gospel of Luke, in addition to the fig tree, other trees are sprouting leaves. Who are these other trees? In 1923, after World War I, the victorious allied nations split the Ottoman Empire into a number of separate countries. Countries that sprouted leaves at around the same time as the fig tree: the Turkish Oak of Turkey, the Cedar of Lebanon, the Olive Tree of Syria, the Pedunculate Oak of Sudan, the Umbrella Thorn of Libya, the Adam's Tree of Iraq, the Cyprus of Iran, and the Oak of Jordan. All of these began sprouting leaves in the 1930's and 1940's, and these are the same countries that come against Israel in Ezekiel 38, the Gog of Magog alliance. That just can't be just coincidence.

The third sign that we are the Final Generation is a sexual identity crisis that human societies are undergoing right before our eyes. People are claiming that there are more than two genders and that marriage is broader than just between a man and a woman. Never before in history have these issues had worldwide acceptance or the force of law behind them. In Luke 17, Jesus said his coming would be like the days of Lot in Sodom and Gomorrah. Is our current sexual identity crisis what He was talking about when He spoke of the days of Lot who lived in a hypersexual culture?

The fourth sign involves technology. And if you were born in the 60's or 70's, I don't have to tell you that everything technological is changing at warp speed compared to the way things used to be. You can see the change; you can almost feel it. Information, the total knowledge known by mankind and the basis of technology is doubling now on a yearly basis. That is just insane. In Dan 12:4, we are told that at the time of the end, knowledge will increase. That is an understatement if it was speaking of today's world.

The impact of this change in technology on the potential for bible prophecy coming true is staggering. The fifth sign is that we are the first generation that can destroy ourselves and our planet. This could happen either environmentally or with nuclear weapons. At the seventh trumpet, the twenty-four elders refer to people who destroy the earth:

> *You should reward Your servants the prophets and the saints, and those who fear Your name, small and great. And should destroy those who destroy the earth.* (Rev 11:18)

At his return, Jesus will punish those destroying the earth. Destroying the earth wasn't possible before, but it is now.

The sixth sign is that we are the first generation with the technology to implement the infamous Mark of The Beast that restricts buying and selling. Digital currency can enforce such a mandate. In 2022, the USA's Federal Reserve began testing a digital dollar. Digital currency will be upon us in a matter of just a few years. Digital currency isn't the Mark, but it is the way to enforce the Mark.

The seventh sign is the internet and the proliferation of cell phones; now to 67% of the entire world's population. This allows the preaching of the gospel to all the ethnic groups in the whole world in a way that was never feasible before. We know from Matt 24 that this gospel of the kingdom shall be preached in the whole world as a testimony to all the nations, and then the end will come. Cell phones will allow this preaching to take place.

Cell phones will also allow other critical end time events like the Abomination of Desolation to be viewed by the entire world's population. Jesus said, "When you *see* the Abomination of Desolation." How would the entire world "see" the abomination without a technology like a cell phone?

You've heard of the "internet of things" that can connect your appliances to the internet, but have you heard about the "internet of souls?" The eighth sign is a technology that someday relatively soon will allow scientists to connect human minds to the internet. Elon Musk believes this event might be possible as soon as 2030.

You may not have thought about it, but this would likely end salvation as we know it for those whose brains are connected. Jesus came to save sinners who repent, not those who have a computer thinking for them. Repentance, faith, love of God and personal choice all require independent thinking. Jesus will not allow this technology to overtake the entire world, He will definitely come back first.

All these signs are pointing to a season, not an exact date, but to a season that is already here. During this season, we will have the opportunity to point to these things to prove the credibility of the Bible to others. As things occur, we can use them to prove the Bible true.

But what are you going to do with this information personally, now you know that Jesus will likely return in the lifetime of you or your children? We are in a dilemma. We are the Final Generation, but it is a generation that isn't aware of the fact because we are asleep. We are a generation of churchgoers who don't think about the return of our Lord on a regular basis, and therefore, miss the signs of His soon return. We are also a generation that doesn't know how to prepare for the return of our Lord. And being ready is everything!

In order to understand how to be ready as Jesus commands, we need to first understand God's Prophetic Plan; His plan from Genesis to Revelation. Once we understand His plan, we can align ourselves with it. This is a primary way that we prepare for the Last Days.

But you might ask, "Isn't God's plan complex?" It is simpler than you think. Let's take a look at it.

CHAPTER SIX

God's Prophetic Plan

God's ways are not our ways.

> *For My thoughts are not your thoughts, nor*
> *are your ways My ways," says the Lord.*
> (Isa 55:8)

Perhaps that is the main reason that we misunderstand God's purposes in the Last Days. As human beings, we would likely organize time and the world much differently than God has. However, in the very next verse in Isaiah, God tells us that his ways and thoughts are *higher* than ours. His prophetic plan for the redemption of the world is perfect. Our fallen intellects don't always grasp that, so God gave us the Bible to help us understand it.

That plan stretches out from Genesis to Revelation. If you have spent time studying the Bible, then you probably recognize that there are four "mountaintops" in God's Plan: *Creation*, *The Fall*, *Salvation*, and *The Consummation* - the return of Jesus.

As we explained in Chapter Two, in *Creation*, God fashioned a paradise where His love for His people could be lived out. God created man and woman and gave them dominion over the earth. In this Eden, He walked with them in the "cool of the day" - in perfect communion and fellowship. It is this relationship that God desires us to return to. And at the completion of his prophetic plan, we will once again see Him face-to-face.

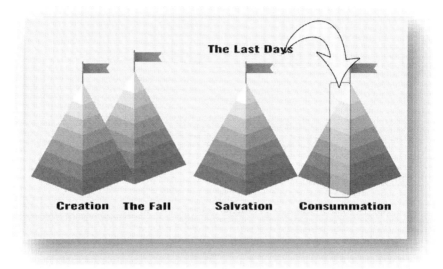

Figure 3: God's Redemptive Timeline

However, as most Christians know, Satan, the serpent, deceived Adam and Eve in the Garden in what we term *The Fall*. And the dominion God gave them over the Earth was handed over to Satan. Additionally, the perfect communion God had with his people was broken. They were cast out of the Garden where they once met God face-to-face.

These are the two things that God desires to restore: man's dominion of the Earth and our face-to-face fellowship with our Lord. All of human history is the unfolding of God's prophetic plan to reestablish these things in a kind of a start-over; a do-over.

In order to accomplish this, God, Himself, came to the Earth in human form in the person of Jesus, the Messiah. And on

Calvary's hill, on a Roman Cross, Jesus paid the debt of all the sins of everyone who had lived and ever would live. This was, and is, our *Salvation*. At the same time, our Lord defeated Satan and his horde of demons and fallen angels.

> *Having disarmed principalities and powers,*
> *He made a public spectacle of them,*
> *triumphing over them in it (the cross)*
> (Col 2:15)

For those who believed and trusted in the finished work of our Savior, God made them a new creation and transferred them from the Kingdom of Darkness (Satan's dominion) into the Kingdom of his beloved son. Jesus, who came to destroy the works of the devil. And from that moment on, everyone who places their complete faith in Jesus will spend all of eternity with Him, the Father, and the Spirit.

Empowering believers with the Spirit was also a major component of the plan God had for us. It is the Spirit who will enable His people to overcome the Last Days.

Yet, despite the fact that "it is finished" (the paying of our sin debt, the defeat of Satan, and empowerment by the Spirit), it isn't done yet. Jesus has defeated sin, but we still sin. And Satan still holds the dominion of this world - Scripture still refers to him as the God of his age:

> *But even if our gospel is veiled, it is veiled to*
> *those who are perishing, whose minds the*
> ***god of this age*** *has blinded* (2 Cor 4:3-4)

The Evil One still holds dominion. And of course, this makes sense. One look at our depraved world and you can see that

Satan still has sway. Jesus is sitting on God's Throne in heaven, but He has yet to sit upon His own throne as King of this world. He receives that title and throne at the 7th Trumpet of Revelation. So one mountaintop event still remains, *The Consummation*, the return of Jesus.

At His return, Jesus will resurrect the dead in Christ, and in the twinkling of an eye, all the living and the resurrected believers will be changed. They will be made like Him, incorruptible. As we discussed in Chapter Two, not only will they be forgiven of their sins, but it will be *impossible* for them to sin. Completely devoid of sin, God's people will once again be able to fellowship with God face-to-face as Adam and Eve once did in the Garden.

Then after the defeat of Satan, the Antichrist, and the False Prophet at the Battle of Armageddon, Jesus will sit upon his glorious throne as the undisputed King of the world. He is my King right now, but at that moment, He becomes everyone's King. The two things God desired to redeem will have been restored.

KEY POINT: *It takes both the Salvation and The Consummation to fully restore the world (and us) to the conditions God created in Eden.*

But what is God's purpose for the end of the age and the Last Days? The Last Days are that highly strategic time period immediately prior to *The Consummation*. It is a time when God will prepare the world for the return of Jesus – and He will use us to accomplish it.

Jesus' cousin, John the Baptist, was given the assignment by God to prepare the land of Israel for the first coming of our

Messiah. You may not realize this, but our task in the Last Days is similar. John the Baptist took his marching orders from the Book of Isaiah:

> *The voice of one crying in the wilderness:*
> *"Prepare the way of the Lord; make straight*
> *in the desert a highway for our God. Every*
> *valley shall be exalted and every mountain*
> *and hill brought low; the crooked places shall*
> *be made straight and the rough places*
> *smooth"* (Isa 40:3-4)

Back in First Century times, if a royal dignitary was visiting a city, he would send his road crew out ahead of him to smooth the road. They would fill in the potholes (exalt every valley) and knock down the high places (every mountain brought low) so their boss would have a smooth road to travel.

John performed this same task to prepare the road for Jesus, but he did it with people not dirt. He uplifted those who were downtrodden, and he rebuked the proud and lofty.

Our role in the Last Days will be *relational* just like John's was; our God-given purpose is to prepare people for the return of the King. We'll uplift the downtrodden, and when appropriate, we'll rebuke the proud. But the essence of our role is that it is people-oriented, not things-oriented. Remember, as we move forward into this book - when we discuss specifics about preparing - those specifics are all about getting people ready to see the King in all His glory. They're what He cares about. They're who He died for.

At all times, but particularly in the Last Days, we are to be ambassadors of a kingdom that is coming.

> We are ambassadors for Christ, as though
> God were pleading through us: 'we implore
> you on Christ's behalf, be reconciled to God'
> (2 Cor 5:20).

At the return of Jesus, the Kingdom of Heaven will invade the kingdoms of this world - but they aren't surrendering without a fight. So, we need to imagine ourselves as God's spies sent ahead into Satan's kingdom. We are here trying to convince as many of his subjects as possible to switch allegiances to the winning side.

As an example, during Joshua's siege of Jericho, the Hebrew leader first sent two spies into the city. They convinced Rahab to switch to God's team. And they promised her, under the influence of the Holy Spirit, that she and everyone who assembled in her house would be saved during the coming battle. She was to hang a scarlet cord, emblematic of the blood of Jesus, in her window as a sign. This is exactly what our role is now. We are to be like those spies asking as many as we can to hang scarlet cords.

So, we are revolutionaries. And here is how we win:

> *They overcame him (Satan) by the blood of*
> *the Lamb and by the word of their testimony,*
> *and they did not love their lives to the death.*
> (Rev 12:11)

It's a really simple 3-part formula. It begins with the Gospel, the blood of the Lamb (Jesus). It involves our testimony or what Jesus has done for us in our lives. And it concludes with us demonstrating to the downtrodden that we love Him (and them) more than the things in our lives or our lives themselves. When all three things line up, what can they say except, "Sign me up for the Jesus team," just as Rahab did.

However, it's that last part of the 3-part formula, not loving our lives to the death, that involves a real cost. A true believer is willing to pay the cost by going to Africa, working in a healthcare practice in a pandemic, taking time to teach a fatherless boy to read, or buying a homeless woman lunch. It might also be something we are asked to die for.

But when the world sees these kinds of things, these sacrifices, they realize that there is something much more powerful than money or politics, something worth dying for themselves. That is how we prepare the way for our King.

But what's so special about the Last Days? How is this different than what we're doing right now? And why does God allow all those calamities to happen? This is one of the great theological questions of all time.

If God's purpose was solely to punish the Earth, then we would be justified in thinking that all we had to do was dig a deep hole and hide. But our purpose in those days has absolutely nothing to do with the type of preparations we would expect unbelievers to make. Hiding in a bunker and eating dried beans is not the type of preparation that Jesus recommends for his followers.

However. it is safe to say that the Last Days will find a lot of people – in fact most people – hiding under rocks, in caves, and in bunkers at some point. This is exactly what Revelation reveals to us:

> And the kings of the earth, the great men, the rich men, the commanders, the mighty men, every slave and every free man, hid themselves in the caves and in the rocks of the mountains, and said to the mountains and rocks, "Fall on us and hide us from the face of Him who sits on the throne and from the wrath of the Lamb!" (Rev 6:15-16)

Imagine sometime in the future when Presidents, Prime Ministers, billionaires, generals, celebrities, the rich and poor alike, will all be hiding in bunkers and caves; hiding from God. It's going to happen. Many of the wealthy are already building bunkers and stocking up on weapons. But that is not what Christians should be doing just prior to those times. No. God has a different purpose and fate for His servants, the true believers. And that purpose can be uncovered by examining what I call the Delay of Jesus.

Have you ever considered why Jesus hasn't returned yet? Why is He delaying? Why did we all endure the pandemic with its sickness, lockdowns, loss of jobs, and the tragedy of losing loved ones? Why didn't Jesus come in 2019 and avoid all that misery? The Apostle Peter gave us an answer that begins like this:

> Knowing this first: that scoffers will come in the last days, walking according to their own

lusts, and saying, "Where is the promise of
His coming? For since the fathers fell asleep,
all things continue as they were from the
beginning of creation." (2 Pet 3:3-4)

According to Peter, unbelievers and believers alike question why Jesus is delaying and whether He is returning at all. Yes, the Bible tells us that in the Last Days, Jesus' delay will cause many to doubt His return. But Peter explains the delay for them and for us:

The Lord is not slack concerning His promise,
as some count slackness, but is longsuffering
toward us, not willing that any should perish
but that all should come to repentance*. But*
the day of the Lord will come as a thief in the
night (2 Pet 3:8-10)

Jesus isn't slow, rather he is patient, not wishing any to perish, desiring all to come to repentance and faith. That patience is what saved you and I. If Jesus had returned in 1900, no one reading (or writing) this book would have been saved. But because of the Grace of God, we were written in the Lamb's Book of Life. Praise the Lord.

But the scriptures are also clear that there will come a day, the Day of the Lord, when Jesus says, "Enough." On that day, everyone who can be saved will have been saved, and there will be no more delay. Then, prior to the wrath of God, He will rescue His own. So it's these souls – these billions of souls that Jesus will redeem – they are the reason Jesus is delaying. And you and I are among them.

But right now, many of those souls are still mocking Jesus, saying, "Where is the promise of his coming?" And as long as nothing significant changes in the lives of these souls, very few will be receptive and open to receiving the Gospel. Therefore, God has a master plan to reach them, to wake them up, and make them understand that life is no longer just "business-as-usual."

KEY POINT: *If nothing significant happens in the lives of unbelievers, most will die without Christ and go to hell.*

In His master plan, God will send a "spiritual hurricane" called the Last Days to disrupt their comfortable lives and make the unbelieving more open to receiving the Gospel. He simply loves them too much to let them go without a fight. Outer bands of catastrophes – like the pandemic and the Ukraine Crisis – are evident in this world already, and the size and strength of these bands will continue to increase.

So, the Last Days are a last chance for the unbelievers to come to faith in Christ. But what about believers? Why are we still here enduring the "spiritual hurricane" along with the unbelievers? The answer is because God has a purpose for us in His master plan. And He will keep us here performing that purpose until it is time for the punishment phase of the "spiritual hurricane." He isn't going to punish his faithful, so right before that punishment or wrath begins, God will rescue His true believers. But until that moment, we have a role to play in the salvation of the lost. If you think preparing for the Last Days is about building a better bunker, it isn't.

KEY POINT: Unbelievers are building bunkers, believers are building the Kingdom.

There is a wonderful book on this subject by my friend and well-known Bible teacher, Joel Richardson, and noted missionary Nathan Graves. The book is called the *Mystery of Catastrophe* (2018). In the book, Mr. Graves recounts what the last several years have been like in Albania, where he and his family have ministered to thousands of escaping Syrian refugees on the road near his church.

Thousands of mostly Muslim people have had their entire lives disrupted. Forced to leave their homes, their jobs, and everything they own, these people had little contact with Christian missionaries before the civil war. But now, through the missionary work of the Graves' church, these souls have been given comfort and spiritual support.

> *I was hungry and you gave Me food; I was*
> *thirsty and you gave Me drink; I was a*
> *stranger and you took Me in; I was naked and*
> *you clothed Me; I was sick and you visited*
> *Me; I was in prison and you came to Me.*
> (Matt 25:35-36)

In the midst of all this pain, hunger, and despair, these blessed missionaries have seen five to seven Muslims *a day* come to faith in Jesus. Now you may not have realized this, but the acts of kindness mentioned in Matt 25 above are actually spoken of in a Last Days context because the passage is from that portion of scripture known as the *Sheep and Goats Judgment,* which occurs upon the return of the Lord.

So, we see that God is permitting and will continue to permit a series of catastrophes – including deception, wars, natural disasters, famine, earthquakes, disease, and persecution – in order to disrupt the lives of unbelievers. It is during and through these disruptions that God's true believers will share the Gospel and the love of Jesus so that all who can be saved will be saved. God has always used disruptions like these to get people's attention. It just so happens that in this case, it will be magnified in the Last Days.

Now, you may be thinking that the Last Days will be a pretty unsafe place for Christians to be. Just think: Jesus will most likely be bringing the very worst of things to your own hometown. But fear not. God will equip those who love Him to do what He desires. And He will protect them as they do it. The Sheep will be ready, but the Goats will hide. Both may attend our churches.

I'm fairly certain that this is new information to you, different from what 99% of Christians have been told to expect from the Last Days. Consider what the angel said to John in the Book of Revelation:

> But **the cowardly**, unbelieving, abominable, murderers, sexually immoral, sorcerers, idolaters, and all liars shall have their part in the lake which burns with fire and brimstone, which is the second death (Rev 21:8)

In this passage, the angel equates being cowardly with all sorts of heinous sins. Why? Because it is a sign of a lack of faith; of not trusting our Lord to provide for and protect us.

But believe it or not, God will use fear for our good. We will discuss this concept further in Chapter Eight.

It is interesting that only two years after we wrote the First Edition of this book, I had a chance to put this aspect into action. In March 2020, the pandemic hit and lockdowns were enforced. You might have forgotten the fear that the virus engendered in those days, but I want you to go back and recall the whole world cowering behind closed doors.

I have a healthcare practice, and our practice had the choice of working through the lockdowns to serve our patients or to protect ourselves and stay in lockdown. Our practice decided to work.

This is what God expects of his servants in these Last Days: to minister to and serve those impacted by the disruptions. And when we do so without fear, we are able to share the Gospel as our practice did many times to those who were shocked that we were willing to risk our own health to care for them.

KEY POINT: *God desires we live fearlessly in the Last Days to present his love to a dying world.*

But God's plans are only half the story of the Last Days. Christians have a great adversary, Satan, who also has a plan for what will take place.

CHAPTER SEVEN

Satan's Plan for the Last Days

We learned in the last chapter that God has a great prophetic plan to save the unrepentant before it is too late. His plan is to allow waves of catastrophe to hit the earth to shake the unsaved out of their comfortable lifestyles. And then for them to be ministered to by Christians who show them the love of Christ and present the Gospel.

However, Satan, the great enemy of Christians, is crafty. He has devised a plan by which he thinks he actually can defeat God himself. He can't do that with power - God is much too powerful. Satan isn't his equal. Satan isn't even the equal of Michael the Archangel who casts him out of heaven (Rev 12:7-9). So, Satan plans to use a legal loophole of sorts.

As we learned in Chapter Six, Satan tricked Adam and Eve into surrendering their dominion over the earth to him. In this way, Satan became the "god" of this age. However, the true God trumped Satan's ploy by coming to earth in the person of Jesus, whose death on the cross won back the dominion and the *Salvation* of everyone who places their faith in Him. And at the *Consummation*, Jesus will be crowned King of the Earth and take the dominion away from Satan forever.

However, as we learned in the last chapter, Jesus is waiting to bring that *Consummation,* and this has bought Satan time to craft one last scheme to try and undo what Jesus accomplished on the cross. Think of Satan as playing a game of chess with God - move and countermove. First God created the world in perfection, then Satan deceived Adam and Eve in a countermove. Jesus then won victory over Satan at the cross, and now Satan plans one more countermove in the Last Days.

At the *Fall,* Satan deceived the only humans on Earth at the time, Adam and Eve. That's how he acquired dominion over it. In the same way, Satan is planning to deceive *every* human on Earth in the Last Days to retake that dominion. This is much more complex than the original deception where there were only two humans; now he has billions to deceive. But Satan knows what is at stake. When Jesus returns, the deceiver will be imprisoned in the abyss (Rev 20:1-3), and it's game over. It's checkmate.

However, as we said, Satan actually thinks he can beat God using this crafty deception. He plans to fool the whole world into signing away their right to repent and be saved – the right that Jesus won for them on the cross. Satan plans to fool the world with the most powerful lie of all time, something known as the Strong Delusion. And he will try to undo the cross with something known as the Mark of the Beast.

You may say, *stop right there*. We aren't going to face the Mark. Whether we are or not, please keep reading. Remember that the Last Days begin like the outer bands of a hurricane, and Satan is already hard at work utilizing those outer bands for this deception. He is laying the groundwork in the media, in government, and even in our churches to prepare people for what is coming. So please continue to read on as it is very relevant to you, your family, and your church. Knowing the enemy's plans in advance is a key strategic advantage.

You have probably heard that the Mark of the Beast is eternal damnation if you take it.

> *If anyone worships the beast and his image,*
> *and receives his mark on his forehead or on*
> *his hand, he himself shall also drink of the*
> *wine of the wrath of God, which is poured out*
> *full strength into the cup of His indignation ...*
> *And the smoke of their torment ascends*
> *forever and ever; and they have no rest day*
> *or night, who worship the beast and his*
> *image, and whoever receives the mark of his*
> *name.* (Rev 14:9-11)

There is no wiggle room in this; the Word says if anyone takes the Mark, they are damned. It is an unforgivable sin. How the Mark changes a person to make them unredeemable isn't completely clear biblically (it may be a genetic change), but it is clear that this is what happens. The Mark is eternal damnation if taken.

When the Mark is instituted, the world will be a completely different spiritual environment than the one we face today. Because of Jesus' victory on the cross, today people can deny Jesus or commit all sorts of sins, but they still have the ability to repent. And if they do, they can still be saved. That's how powerful and important the cross is. However, once the Mark of the Beast is introduced, Satan will have a tool to "undo" the cross for those he deceives into taking it.

You probably think this sounds like "selling your soul to the devil," And that is exactly what it is. Although this is a popular phrase in culture right now, it's currently not possible. People still have the ability to repent. But when the Mark of the Beast is instituted, people who take it will be changed somehow and lose the right Jesus bought them on the cross.

Satan is no fool, he is doing this for a reason. You see, if every *living* person on earth takes the Mark and signs away their right to redemption, there will be no one left on earth for Jesus to come back to. Satan will be able to say to God, "See? They want me as their king, not You." By means of the Mark of the Beast, Satan will have prevented the *Consummation,* he will prevent Jesus from coming back. He will have retained dominion over the earth. And rather than a checkmate by God, it will be a stalemate. Satan will be happy with that.

Of course, not everyone is going to take this horrid Mark. So, Satan plans to eliminate everyone who doesn't take it to create a pure "race" of the unredeemable. This elimination is the Great Tribulation – the hunting down and killing of everyone not deceived into taking the Mark of the Beast. If Satan is successful, he will have a world that is 100% corrupted. And Scripture tells us Satan is going to come pretty close to doing just that. In Matt 24:22, Jesus tells us he has to cut short the days of the Great Tribulation in order that some flesh might be saved. It's going to be a pretty close call. Satan is almost going to win.

The Mark of the Beast is Satan's biggest weapon but it isn't his biggest deception. The Mark of the Beast will be "in your face" - a clear denunciation of God and His right to a person's soul and spirit. That's a tough pill for anyone to swallow. So, Satan has to convince the people of the world to take it – to sign away their right to salvation. He is going to use deception to do that; something the Bible refers to as the Strong Delusion:

> *The coming of the lawless one is according to the working of Satan, with all power, signs, and lying wonders, and with all unrighteous deception among those who perish, because they did not receive the love of the truth, that they might be saved. And for this reason, God will send them strong delusion, that they should believe **the lie**.* (2 Thess 2:9-11)

The Bible calls the Strong Delusion: *the* Lie – the greatest lie of all time. It will convince most people to take the Beast's Mark and worship him. This is the main reason that the Last Days are not "business as usual." Satan will pull out all the stops at that time to achieve his plan, and only those with strong faith will be able to overcome it.

But how does this apply to you and me today? In science labs, in governments, and in the media, Satan is probably preparing the Lie right now. And we may all live to see it unveiled. We don't know exactly what it will be, the Bible doesn't tell us, but here are some ideas.

The Lie might be a medical/genetic advance; a false promise that we can achieve eternal life scientifically without Jesus. Many people would take a Mark to achieve that.

It might be a technological advance; that we can hook our brains up to a computer and know everything. Many people might take a Mark to achieve that.

It might even border on science fiction. Satan and his fallen angels might appear on earth in the guise of "aliens" saying they are the ones who created life on earth, not God, and that they have all the answers to our earthly problems.

I know what you're thinking. These ideas are "tin hat" crazy. But don't laugh these wild sounding ideas off just yet. We know the Strong Delusion will be *the* Lie, the greatest lie of all time. We need to be prepared for a lie of incredible proportions. And media stories about these specific things, transhumanism and aliens, already pepper the airways. All three of these options also echo Satan's original seductive lies to Eve in the Garden: "You will be like God, and surely you won't die." If they worked for Satan once, he will likely try the same lies again in a new, modern form.

Let's look at the Greek behind the passage about the Lie because it confirms this theory that the Strong Delusion is going to be unusual and unexpected. In verse 9, we learn that the coming of the man of sin is in accord with the "working" of Satan. This word translated "working" is the Greek word "energeian," which is the word from which we get our English word "energy." In the New Testament, energeian is always a supernatural working, either from God or the Devil. Then in verse 11, just two verses later, Paul uses this word again when he describes the Strong Delusion. The word translated "strong" is this same word "energeian" or supernatural working. So, the Strong Delusion is actually a supernatural delusion - not a man-created delusion. It comes from Satan and his fallen angels.

Are our churchgoers prepared to face such a supernatural deception? Do they even know that such a thing is coming? It will be a deception that is powerful enough to cause many of those sitting in the pews next to us to walk away from their faith. Paul calls this *the* falling away, the greatest apostasy of all time:

> *Now, brethren, concerning the coming of our Lord Jesus Christ and our gathering together to Him ... that Day will not come unless the falling away comes first* (2 Thess 2:1-3)

Notice it comes before our gathering together to Him – it's prior to any Rapture. So regardless of what end time theories you hold, it is likely that many reading this book will live to see the Lie.

Again, we ask, how prepared are those in your church for this kind of delusion? If they aren't prepared, how will they react when things like a chance for eternal life provided "scientifically" or a chance at knowing what a computer knows are presented to them? These temptations will be very attractive to all but those with the strongest faith.

As 2 Thess 2:9-11 indicates, God's solution to the Lie is simple: He has given His followers *the truth* to protect us. The truth is the Word of God and the Holy Spirit who helps us understand and interpret it. Those who receive the truth are saved.

*We should no longer be children, tossed to and fro and carried about with every wind of doctrine, by the trickery of men, in the cunning craftiness of deceitful plotting, but, speaking **the truth** in love, may grow up in all things into Him who is the head—Christ (Eph 4:14-15)*

We are to overcome trickery, cunning, craftiness, and deceitful plotting by speaking the truth in the context of the loving environment of our churches and small groups. "Speaking the truth in love" is often misapplied as gently calling out someone who has sinned, but as we see in its context, it is about overcoming bad doctrine and deceit. Our churches' protection against the Strong Delusion is to teach the truth.

Satan, of course, knows this. So, he is going to do everything in his unrighteous power to prevent the love of the truth from growing within people and protecting them. That is the struggle of the Last Days. It is a struggle over truth.

Key Point: preparing for the Last Days is, at its heart, knowing and understanding this eternal struggle between God and Satan over the teaching of the truth.

And that struggle has already begun. God has placed instructions in His Word which are truth. Believers who love this truth will trust God and overcome the evil one in the Last Days.

However, Satan is attempting to deceive churchgoers to not love this truth or to not understand it. As an example, we saw in Chapters Four and Five that the Bible has instructed us to be watchful for signs of the Last Days, but most Christians are not being watchful. This is Satan's doing. God's Word on this matter is clear, but Satan deceives us as to it's true meaning or distracts us from reading the Word at all. And the impact of this deception and distraction is that the vast majority of churchgoers will still be asleep when the Strong Delusion, *the* Lie, is unleashed. Because of this, many will be foolish virgins who do not enter the wedding feast.

In many other ways, Satan is trying to deceive believers right now. As you continue to read this book, keep this in mind. You are *already* engaged in a battle during the Last Days. It is a struggle for your mind; a struggle for truth.

God, however, is not going to be outplayed by Satan. He plans to use the catastrophes of the Last Days in one more way. A positive way that may surprise you.

CHAPTER EIGHT

Fear

We began discussing the concept of "fear" in Chapter Two. But reading the previous chapters about the plans of God and Satan has probably left you feeling somewhat uncomfortable. Waves of catastrophe and strong delusions sound frightening even to those with the strongest faith. Some feel guilty about being afraid, but we shouldn't be. Fear is a normal human emotion, why else would the Bible be filled with admonitions to "fear not" - if those hearing the advice weren't afraid? All of us feel fear occasionally.

Fear and anxiety can paralyze us. And unfortunately, no one will be able to escape fear in this sinful and broken world, especially in the Last Days. It's real. It can be paralyzing. However, the main issue God wants us to wrestle with is where we *go* when we're afraid. Where do you take your fears? How we deal with them is crucial to our Christian walk because God plans to use fear to transform us. How is He going to do that? He will use the most powerful force on the planet to accomplish this: Himself.

> *God is our refuge and strength, a very present help in trouble, therefore we will not fear, even though the earth be removed, and though the mountains be carried into the midst of the sea; though its waters roar and be troubled, though the mountains shake with its swelling.* (Psalm 46:1-3)

Psalm 46 is one of Christianity's most beloved Psalms. It was dedicated "for the virgins (alamoth in Hebrew)." Yes, like the ten virgins of the parable; the virgins present in the Last Days. And certainly, the events of Psalm 46 sound like Last Days' catastrophes. We could paraphrase these verses in modern day terms: "even though there are pandemics, riots, Ukraine Wars, runaway inflation, and nuclear explosions …" So, this Psalm is for us and for these days.

God explains He is a very present help in our troubles. He is all-knowing, the Last Days don't surprise Him; He is all-powerful, nothing will happen to us that He doesn't allow and can't overcome; and He is all-present, He will be right there with us as things are happening. He can and will strengthen and protect us throughout all these days.

Remembering God's omnipresent power transforms our fear into faith. Psalm 46 concludes like this:

> *Be still, and know that I am God; I will be exalted among the nations, I will be exalted in the earth! The LORD of hosts is with us; the God of Jacob is our refuge.* (Psalm 46:10-11)

We defeat fear when we allow God to calm our anxious minds by remembering that the Lord of hosts is with us and all-powerful – He is God - and He wins in the end.

KEY POINT: Fear can be defined as overwhelming circumstances *without* God, while faith is overwhelming circumstances *with* God.

In both situations, fear and faith, there are overwhelming circumstances. The difference is remembering God is completely in control of them. Faith is trusting in that knowledge and acting accordingly.

Fear, in and of itself isn't bad. It's an emotion that God created and gave to us to remind us to trust Him! When we feel that surge of adrenaline in our system, it is a signal for us to pray and rely on Him. When we do, and trust that He is the all-powerful God, He gives us the power to be still in the midst of trouble. Fear is only a sin when we neglect to lean on the power of God and allow it to control us.

In the Parable of the Ten Virgins that we discussed earlier, what differences were there between the wise virgins who enter heaven with Jesus and those who are shut out of heaven? The wise virgins were ready for the bridegroom's return; they brought oil for their lamps. The Greek word translated "lamps" actually means torches, so these were big, bright lamps and are probably symbolic of the testimony of our lives – what we say and do as evidence of our faith. Oil is universally a symbol for the Holy Spirit.

The wise virgins had this oil, and their testimony stayed lit even during the scariest parts of the Last Days. They relied on God despite their initial fear, and that reliance transformed their fear into faith. God rewarded this faith by bringing them into the wedding feast (heaven).

The foolish virgins ran out of oil, and as a result their testimony fizzled out. They neglected to rely on God and allowed their fear to control them. This is evidence they were never truly saved. They may have thought they were – they were waiting for the bridegroom after all – but they weren't really "in Christ."

This explanation may upset you. Perhaps you realize that you aren't as fearless as you should be, that you sometimes allow overwhelming circumstances to get the best of you. You may worry that maybe you aren't truly saved. If this is your worry, be comforted. Understand that God is forming all of us into His image, and none of us are there yet. In fact, God is allowing the Last Days for this purpose – to more fully form us. He uses fearful situations as a means to do just that. God does this routinely, but He will use the Last Days and its waves of catastrophe to intensify the process. How does that work?

The epistle of James speaks of how trials and testing transform a person, "*Knowing that the testing of your faith produces patience* (James 1:3)." In this verse, the Greek word translated "testing" is dokimion, which in the first century was a test to prove something genuine.

The picture is of a goldsmith heating a mass of impure gold until it melts. At that point, the impurities come to surface, and the goldsmith then skims them off leaving a pure metal. That is what hard times do for us. The "heat" of trials transforms us into the genuine. This is why James would precede this verse with what seems like a crazy statement:

> *My brethren, **count it all joy** when you fall into various trials* (James 1:2)

Not only do waves of adversity have a purpose in bringing others to Christ as we learned in the Chapter Six, James also tells us we are to count these outer bands of the spiritual hurricane as a blessing because they transform us. That seems foolish in our comfort-driven culture, but God uses fear and adversity to bring out the genuine Christian in us, to make us complete in Christ.

The picture James paints is similar to exercise. Exercise builds muscle and endurance, and although most don't like the work that exercise entails, it has the positive impact of getting us in shape. Overcoming fearful trials builds spiritual muscle and spiritual endurance. Here is what Paul says about this type of training:

> Let us run with **endurance** the race that is set
> before us, looking unto Jesus, the author and
> finisher of our faith, who for the joy that was
> set before Him **endured** the cross, despising
> the shame, and has sat down at the right
> hand of the throne of God. (Heb 12:1-2)

Developing endurance is like training for long distance running. And Jesus is our model and mentor. His endurance exceeded anything we can imagine. The end result of this is that we are perfected and made more like Him. This is what the Church calls sanctification. It is an ongoing activity.

So, the Last Days help us be transformed, but what kind of transformation is God looking for? Besides becoming faithful, He is transforming us into those who can love:

> Beloved, let us love one another, for love is of
> God; and everyone who loves is born of God
> and knows God. He who does not love does
> not know God, for God is love. (1 John 4:7-8)

God is love; this is His very nature. By transforming us to love, He is making us more like Himself. This echoes Jesus' greatest commandments: to love God and love others. As we learned in the last chapters, loving others and sharing the Gospel with them is God's plan for the Last Days.

Second, God is transforming us to be purified by the power of the Holy Spirit to live in obedience – to reflect the image of our Creator:

> If you love Me (you will)] keep My
> commandments. (John 14:15)

Jesus shows that if we love Him, His Spirit will empower and enable us to keep His other commands. A few verses later, Jesus flips this around:

> If you keep My commandments, you will
> abide in My love (John 15:10)

God is a Holy God. By purifying ourselves, we are able to abide in Him and have a relationship to him.

All these transformations happen within our minds. I was saved when I was 33 years old. Prior to that, my brain was wired by Satan's lies told to me by the news media, the government, and yes, even by my parents and friends. Over my life I've had to disconnect from all those falsehoods and connect to the truth of the Bible.

> Do not be conformed to this world, but be
> transformed by the renewing of your mind,
> that you may prove what is that good and
> acceptable and perfect will of God.
> (Rom 12:2)

In order to be transformed, believers have to first disconnect from Satan's lies fed to them by our culture. Believers then have to replace those sources of information with a better source. We have to transform our minds with the truth of the Gospel and the Word of God. If we are not being transformed, if we are not overcoming fear, perhaps one reason is that we are not renewing our minds. Old lies produce the same old results. But when we are renewed, we can know what God's will is, His perfect will.

Imagine how important knowing God's will is in the Last Days when Satan will be promoting the Strong Delusion! All of us need to be rewiring our minds daily with the Word of God to overcome the evil that is coming.

> KEY POINT: Studying the Bible daily isn't just something "nice to do," but is the means of rewiring our brains.

As we mentioned in the last chapter, the Last Days is a battle for your mind. Rewiring your mind with the Word of God is a critical part of loving the truth, turning fear into faith, and preparing for those days.

"Culture eats strategy for breakfast" is a famous quote from legendary management consultant and writer Peter Drucker. By this he means that who we are and who we are becoming is more important than the strategies we employ. This is dramatically true in the Last Days. As we prepare for those days, we need to focus on our becoming people who trust God – who trust in the blessed hope – who are those who have faith. Jesus said those with the faith of a mustard seed could move mountains. Developing faith is a primary way we prepare for the Last Days.

We realize this chapter has presented challenging thoughts. Perhaps they have made you question whether or not you are being transformed as you should be. If so, take a moment now to repent. (Repent means to turn.) And confess to God that you want to turn from wickedness to purity; from selfishness to love, from fear to sharing His message. All of us can improve in these areas. Ask for the infilling of His Holy Spirit to help you as you practice these things from now on.

KEY POINT: *The Last Days are our chance to be transformed by the Spirit into the persons that Jesus wants us to be.*

But what about those attending our churches who aren't being transformed by the outer bands of difficulty? What about those who instead leave whatever belief they had behind and walk away from Jesus?

This is one of the most difficult aspects of the Last Days to consider. As we spoke of in Chapter Six, there is a Great Apostasy coming. Jesus, Himself, said half of the Kingdom of Heaven will be foolish virgins at the time of His return. This breaks my heart, just as it did Jesus' heart. He spent a great deal of time during His final week of life warning the foolish virgins of their impending fate.

CHAPTER NINE

Is the Church at Risk?

What a person shares during their last precious hours of life is usually a very important message. If you are a leader of some sort, it frequently is the core ideas of your organization – the most important message you want to get across.

As we stated in Chapter Three, during Jesus' last week of life before his betrayal and crucifixion, He shared what He really wanted us to know about the Last Days. He warned churchgoers about the very real risk of them going to Hell. And he did this over and over and over again. He didn't warn us once or twice, but in practically every parable and sermon he delivered.

These warnings weren't given primarily to those living worldly lifestyles. Most were given to those who thought they were following God. Jesus calls them servants of the Master or virgins trying to keep themselves pure. They call him Lord and even perform miracles. They are the ones waiting for the return of the bridegroom. Yet a lot of these well-meaning folks end up in Hell.

We now know from Chapter Seven that Satan's Strong Delusion is the reason for this risk to churchgoers. It is a Lie so convincing that if you do not love the truth, you will not endure it. Look what Jesus had to say about this:

> *For false christs and false prophets will rise*
> *and show great signs and wonders to*
> *deceive, if possible, even the elect.* ***See, I have***
> ***told you beforehand****.* (Matt 24:24-25)

This is a pretty sober warning. On Sunday, look out over your congregation. In the Parable of the Ten Virgins, Jesus told us only half of those waiting for His return are ready to enter the wedding feast!! That would mean only half your congregation is truly saved. The other half will be taken in by the Strong Delusion. Let that sink in.

Getting ready for the return of Jesus is a salvation issue. Are our churches sharing this same message? Do our churches even believe this? And most importantly, what can we do to help prevent this horrible fate for our fellow churchgoers?

Let's begin by looking at the parables and illustrations Jesus gave during that last week and see just how serious he says not being ready for his return is. In the Parable of the Wedding Feast, look what happens to the guest who wasn't properly dressed:

> *But when the king came in to see the guests,*
> *he saw a man there who did not have on a*
> *wedding garment. So he said to him, 'Friend,*
> *how did you come in here without a wedding*
> *garment?' And he was speechless. Then the*
> *king said to the servants, 'Bind him hand and*
> *foot, take him away, and cast him into outer*
> *darkness; there will be weeping and gnashing*
> *of teeth'* (Matt 22:11-13)

The unwelcome guest thought he belonged at the feast, but instead he is cast into outer darkness. He thought he was saved, but obviously he wasn't. In the Last Days, many will think they are going to heaven and will be disappointed.

In the Parable of the Head of the Household, Jesus speaks to those whom He has set in charge of His household:

> But know this, that if the master of the house had known what hour the thief would come, he would have watched and not allowed his house to be broken into. Therefore, you also be ready, for the Son of Man is coming at an hour you do not expect. (Matt 24:43-44)

Who is the "master of the house?" They are those Jesus has set in authority over his flock. Some are fathers or mothers. Some are small group leaders or Sunday school teachers. Some are pastors, some are seminary presidents, and some are the leaders of denominations. Nearly all of us carry some level of responsibility.

And Jesus tells us that if we are not watchful, our house will be broken into and robbed. That means that those Jesus has given to us: children, students, congregations, or entire denominations may go to Hell rather than be saved if we are not watchful for His return. That is a sobering thought. This makes watching and knowing if we are in the Final Generation imperative.

In this passage Jesus also said, "You also be ready." This is all-inclusive. Even if you aren't convinced that we are the Final Generation, Jesus wants you to prepare as if we are!

When Jesus shared that He is coming at an hour no one expects, He said this to warn people that it might be *sooner* than they expected. Yet every single time I hear this quoted, it is said in such a way as to imply Jesus will come *later* than we think – as a caution against date setting the return of the Lord. Now we absolutely shouldn't date set, but do you realize how this caution against date setting has actually reversed Jesus' true meaning? Rather than an encouragement to get ready now, most use it as an excuse not to think about Jesus' return.

KEY POINT: *Jesus tells us all of us must get ready for His return NOW - regardless of our opinions.*

Jesus continues the parable and describes two of these servants of the master whom He set in charge of his household: one wise and one wicked. Look what He says about the wicked servant:

> *The master of that servant will come on a day when he is not looking for him and at an hour that he is not aware of, and will cut him in two and appoint him his portion with the hypocrites. There shall be weeping and gnashing of teeth.* (Matt 24:50-51)

This servant of the master who is punished was a leader, one Jesus put in charge of His household. Maybe it's even a president of a denomination. Yet, despite all his credentials, this leader is unsaved, and Jesus cuts him in two - YIKES. This parable deserves a closer look to see why this Christian leader is punished.

> *But if that evil servant says in his heart, 'My*
> *master is delaying his coming,' and begins to*
> *beat his fellow servants, and to eat and drink*
> *with the drunkards* (Matt 24:48-49)

The genesis of this man's sin is that he says in his heart that Jesus is "delaying His coming." How can that be a sin? Jesus has delayed His coming for almost 2000 years! So, we need to think about this carefully. Is it possible this leader doesn't think he is part of the Final Generation when he *should* have known? Is it possible that he says to himself that Jesus might not return in a hundred years, even though the evidence that Jesus is coming sooner is apparent?

KEY POINT: *The genesis of many Last Days sins will be thinking that Jesus isn't coming soon.*

Jesus then explains that this lack of understanding of scripture (The Fig Tree Parable) and a lack of understanding of world events leads to a host of sins. Thinking he has all the time in the world, this leader neglects to love his fellow churchgoers and even mistreats them. Might part of this mistreating of his flock be that he doesn't help them prepare for the Last Days? The lesson Jesus is getting across is that we do not have all the time in the world. It is essential to know that we are in the Final Generation and to begin to prepare.

In this parable, there is also a wise and faithful servant that we should emulate:

> *Who then is a faithful and wise servant,*
> *whom his master made ruler over his*
> *household, to give them food in due season?*

95

Blessed is that servant whom his master,
when he comes, will find so doing. Assuredly,
I say to you that he will make him ruler over
all his goods. (Matt 24:45-47)

You probably noticed that this faithful servant is serving his flock right up until the return of Jesus – and Jesus rewards him for it. But you may not have noticed that this is a riddle of sorts. Jesus asked, "Who?" Who is the faithful and wise servant? Jesus gave us three clues: he is a slave (the Greek word translated "servant" actually means slave), he is put in charge of his maters house, and he provides food for the household at a special time. Who in the Old Testament fits these criteria?

Why it's Joseph! Joseph was sold into slavery, was put in charge of Potiphar's household, and provided food for his father's household and all of Egypt during the famine. Only Joseph fits Jesus' clues.

> KEY POINT: *Jesus is telling us to be like Joseph in the Last Days.*

"Wait a minute!", you might be saying. "Does Jesus expect us to be preppers in the Last Days?" I'm sure visions of crazy people hiding in bunkers are entering your thoughts right now. And no, we already discussed how it is the unsaved who hide in the Last Days. But keep this thought about putting food away in mind, because we'll discuss it more in Chapter Thirteen.

But "food" can also mean spiritual food. And certainly, Jesus expects all of us to share His Word right up until His return, and that is something all of us should be doing.

The next parable Jesus told his disciples was the Parable of the Ten Virgins which we have discussed at length elsewhere in this book. In this parable, all ten are virgins, attempting to be pure, and all are awaiting the return of their bridegroom, Jesus. But look what he says to those who don't keep their lamps lit:

> *And while they went to buy, the bridegroom came, and those who were **ready** went in with him to the wedding; and the door was shut. Afterward the other virgins came also, saying, 'Lord, Lord, open to us!' But he answered and said, 'Assuredly, I say to you, I do not know you.'* (Matt 25:10-12)

Again, as in each of the previous parables, there is a separation of the saved from the unsaved. However, in each case, all of the people thought they were among God's chosen. They were servants of the master or virgins. Yet, not all were saved. In this parable, only 50% were saved. That is a destressing percentage. If only 50% of those in the pews of your church are saved, we all have work to do.

What is it that causes Jesus to shut the door on these unfortunate, foolish virgins?

> *And at midnight a cry was heard: 'Behold, the bridegroom is coming; go out to meet him!' Then all those virgins arose and trimmed their lamps. And the foolish said to the wise, 'Give us some of your oil, for our lamps are going out.' But the wise answered, saying, 'No, lest there should not be enough for us*

and you; but go rather to those who sell, and
buy for yourselves (Matt 25:6-9)

The first theme of this parable is the suddenness of the Last Days; the foolish virgins don't have enough time to gather the oil needed to keep their lamps lit. Jesus is telling us if we aren't ready when the warning sounds, churchgoers won't have time to prepare. They need to prepare now. A spiritual hurricane is coming upon the world. You can't climb a ladder and put up the storm shutters when the wind is already blowing at 75 miles per hour!

KEY POINT: *The time to prepare for the Last Days is right now.*

The second theme of this wonderful parable is the concept of Jesus not knowing the foolish virgins. This is similar to another prophecy Jesus told earlier in his ministry where He had this to say to some of his followers upon his return:

Not everyone who says to Me, 'Lord, Lord,'
shall enter the kingdom of heaven, but he
who does the will of My Father in heaven.
Many will say to Me in that day, 'Lord, Lord,
have we not prophesied in Your name, cast
out demons in Your name, and done many
wonders in Your name?' And then I will
declare to them, 'I never knew you; depart
from Me, you who practice lawlessness!'
(Matt 7:21-23)

So, calling Jesus, "Lord," and doing works in his Name isn't enough to be ready for his return. I don't know about you, but I have never cast out demons or prophesied. Those are pretty impressive works, but even doing miracles is not enough to qualify someone for the wedding feast.

Despite their works, Jesus never knew these people; He didn't have a relationship with them. The reason might be that they practiced lawlessness. They didn't occasionally sin as all people do, but they continually sinned; they practiced sinning.

> No one who lives in him keeps on sinning. No one who continues to sin has either seen him or known him. (1 John 3:6 NIV)

Continual, unabated sin without repentance is a sign that a person was never saved to begin with.

Jesus then shared the famous Parable of the Talents. In this parable, the master gives a great treasure to three of his trusted servants. What is Jesus' *greatest* treasure? Why the Gospel, of course. But look at what happens to the servant of the master who hides this great treasure upon this master's return:

> So take the talent from him, and give it to him who has ten talents ... And cast the unprofitable servant into the outer darkness. There will be weeping and gnashing of teeth.' (Matt 25: 28-30)

Just as in each of the previous parables, a contrast is set up between the saved and unsaved. All three servants thought they were serving their master, but only two truly were. But why was this servant being punished?

> *I was afraid, and went and hid your talent in the ground.* (Matt 25: 25)

The servant was afraid to invest the great treasure he was given, in our opinion, the Gospel. He was frightened at what might happen if he did. His fear is a sign that he likely didn't have the Spirit or faith to trust God.

Our world is rapidly darkening. It is likely in the near future that it won't only be unpopular to share the Gospel, it might become illegal. You might not only get de-platformed from Facebook or YouTube, you might go to jail. So overcoming this fear by means of the power of the Spirit within us is something to practice right now. Yes, they can throw you into prison like they did Paul, but maybe that gives you even a wider audience to testify to.

And we should be encouraged that the other two servants in this parable did share the great treasure they were given. They each doubled what they were given. Lord, may that be said of us someday.

KEY POINT: *Jesus expects us to share His great treasure, the Gospel, even when it's dangerous or illegal.*

The final illustration Jesus shared that week was the Prophecy of the Sheep and Goats. Look at what happens to those who call Jesus, "Lord," but choose to not care for the least and the lowest.

> *Then he will answer them, saying, 'Truly, I say to you, as you did not do it to one of the least of these, you did not do it to me. And these*

*will go away into eternal punishment, but the
righteous into eternal life.* (Matt 25:45-46)

In the earlier chapter about the purpose of the Last Days,
we discussed what those things that the righteous did for
the least of these, but that the unrighteous neglected:

*Then the righteous will answer Him, saying,
'Lord, when did we see You hungry and feed
You, or thirsty and give You drink? When did
we see You a stranger and take You in, or
naked and clothe You? Or when did we see
You sick, or in prison, and come to You?* (Matt
25:37-39)

In Chapter Six about God's purpose for the Last Days, we
discussed how during those times God will force all people
out of their comfortable lives by means of deception, war,
famine, natural disasters, disease, and persecution. When
that happens, we need to come alongside them to feed and
clothe them, visit them in prison, and love them as Jesus
would. That is God's plan for the Last Days. And it is a basis
of how Jesus will judge people because it reflects their level
of faith.

As you have been reading this book, I am sure a theme is
beginning to become apparent: those with the Spirit share
the love of Christ and the Gospel regardless of social
pressure or danger. Those without the Spirit (the unsaved)
are frightened to do so. Many sitting to your left and right in
church may fall into this second category. Not everyone
who thinks they are saved, truly are. Jesus' parables told

during His last week of life that we presented in this chapter confirm this.

Although loving and sharing the Gospel with others outside of our churches is God's plan for the Last Days, many of our churches are currently ill equipped for it, and many to our left and to our right in the pews are just as lost as those outside the church. So, a major part of our responsibility, in fact our *first* responsibility in the Last Days, is to work along with the Spirit to move those in the second category, the unsaved within our churches, into the Kingdom of God through love, prayer, and good works. We cannot love and serve the world until we love our serve our fellow churchgoers.

KEY POINT: *We need to love, pray for, and serve the unsaved in our own churches.*

But what would happen if your church decided to preach these warnings found in this chapter to your congregation next week – without having prepared them in advance? It might wake up some of those in the pews, wouldn't it? I can imagine everyone serious about Jesus would be asking "What do I need to do to get ready?" However, everyone not serious might get up and leave. It reminds me of John Chapter 6 where Jesus preached a very difficult message.

> *After this many of his disciples turned back and no longer walked with him. So, Jesus said to the twelve, 'Do you want to go away as well?'* (John 6:66-67)

Jesus, of course, had a big advantage on your Pastor. Being God, He knew who would never be saved; and it only strengthened his followers by having the unrepentant leave. However, in our churches, we don't have that advantage. We need to try to bring them *all* to the Kingdom and let Jesus decide later who is saved and who isn't.

But how can we best accomplish that? How can we present this urgent message from Jesus without scaring off the seekers in our pews?

Well, it might sound a bit self-serving, but those of us in Last Days Overcomers have spent a lifetime of ministry preparing to do just that. A one-day conference by our group, or a similar group, in your town might be just the kickoff they need to begin to prepare for the Last Days. And just the kickoff some need to begin a new life in Christ. Our contact information is on page vii at the beginning of the book.

CHAPTER TEN

Ambiguity About the Last Days

We just learned in the last chapter that Jesus has said that many churchgoers will be ill-prepared for the coming Last Days. Although that is so generally, it doesn't mean you or I have to be ill-prepared. So how should we get ready? I think at this point in the book, most readers will agree that we need to do something to get ready, but what?

The problem with preparing is that we have many conflicting theories of what the Last Days will look like. What should we get ready for: your theory, my theory, or the next guy's theory? There are so many ideas about what will happen, most throw up their hands in confusion. It would be so nice if God took a highlight pen and marked those passages He thought were most important.

Actually, He did something very similar. He told us to "not be ignorant" of four main Last Days ideas - four things we were not to be "dumb" about - four things we could hang our hats on. If God tells us not to ignore four things, shouldn't we be absolutely sure to understand and know these things? We should read and study the whole Bible, but if God takes the time to point out four things and says, "don't be ignorant about these things," then we should be *extra* diligent about them. What is sad, however, is these are the very portions of scripture that much of the Church has gotten wrong. There are, of course, historical reasons for this confusion. Consider the following example.

105

The nation of Israel was invaded in AD 70 and AD 133. Jerusalem was leveled to the ground, the Jewish people scattered all over the world, and by Roman decree, the people weren't allowed back into Israel. At that point, the Romans had had enough of Jewish revolts and didn't want another. They even renamed the land, "Palestine," so the name of Israel would not exist.

Now imagine you are a believer in the Fifth Century, and you're reading your Bible about the Last Days. You see all these references to Israel and a Last Days' Temple. What would you think? Naturally everyone back then wondered, "How will this be fulfilled without a nation of Israel or a temple?" They knew the Bible wasn't in error, so some imagined God had replaced Israel with the Church. This is how "replacement theology" came into being. People assumed that God was done with Israel.

But then as we learned in Chapter Four, Israel was miraculously recreated as a nation in 1948. This was the first and greatest sign of the Last Days that Jesus gave us - the fig tree began sprouting leaves. And suddenly, prophecies that once seemed impossible had the ability to come true – Israel existed again. So, it is not surprising that the first thing God wants us to not be ignorant of is His Last Days plan for Israel.

> For **I do not desire, brethren, that you should be ignorant of this mystery**, lest you should be wise in your own opinion, that blindness in part has happened to Israel until the fullness of the Gentiles has come in. And so all Israel will be saved, as it is written: "The Deliverer

*will come out of Zion, And He will turn away
ungodliness from Jacob; For this is My
covenant with them, When I take away their
sins."* (Rom 11:25-27)

God wants us to know that unsaved Israel is spiritually-
blind. We shouldn't be surprised that they are rejecting
Jesus today, but the day is coming when all of Israel that
survives the Great Tribulation will be saved. God loves and
cares for them. And if he does, so should we.

KEY POINT: God still loves unsaved Israel and has a plan for
them in the Last Days. We should love them also.

The second thing that God doesn't want us to be ignorant of
is typology, that what happened in the Old Testament is a
picture of what will happen again in the Last Days.

*Moreover, brethren, **I do not want you to be
unaware (ignorant)** that all our fathers were
under the cloud, all passed through the sea ...
Now all these things happened to them as
examples, and they were written for our
admonition, upon whom the ends of the ages
have come.* (1 Cor 10:1, 11)

Some churches say that we should unhinge ourselves from
the Old Testament. But God says we should not be ignorant
of it or ignore it. In the Gospel of Luke for instance, Jesus
told us his return would be like the days of Noah and the
days of Lot in Sodom. We need to heed His instruction. God
gave us pictures, Old Testament "types" to inform us, and
the concept is reenforced by Jesus himself.

The third thing God wants us to not be ignorant of is His timing.

> **But, beloved, be not ignorant of this one thing**, that one day is with the Lord as a thousand years, and a thousand years as one day. The Lord is not slack concerning His promise, as some count slackness, but is long suffering toward us, not willing that any should perish but that all should come to repentance. But the day of the Lord will come as a thief in the night. (2 Pet 3:8-9)

People often ask, "Why does God permit pain and suffering in this world? If He loves us, why doesn't He solve the problem?" What these folks often miss is that sinful humans are the problem. And in order to eliminate the problem, God would have to eliminate them. But he is patient, wanting them and everyone else who is unsaved to come to repentance before punishment sweeps them away.

This reenforces the importance of evangelism in God's plan. God is delaying His return for the sole purpose of giving the unsaved another chance. We should help this effort.

This brings us to the final thing that God wants us not be ignorant of: the Resurrection.

> But **I do not want you to be ignorant, brethren, concerning those who have fallen asleep**, lest you sorrow as others who have no hope. ... and the dead in Christ will rise first. (1 Thess 4:13, 16)

The resurrection of the dead in Christ is our blessed hope. And God wants us to focus on it for two reasons. First, so we don't sorrow about our loved ones who have passed on. And second because even if we die ourselves, a resurrection is coming! This is one of the greatest keys to the Last Days. No matter what the world does to our friends and family, or even to us during this difficult time, its temporary. Jesus is bringing all the souls of the dead in Christ with him when he returns and they will rise and resurrect.

This knowledge allows you to live fearlessly. You are invincible until the day God decides that you should die. The world cannot kill you if God has destined you to survive until the Rapture. And if He hasn't destined you to live, He has chosen this other course for your good. We can trust Him whatever happens.

KEY POINT: Knowledge of the Resurrection should make us live fearlessly in the Last Days.

So, these four things: Israel, typology of the Old Testament, God's timing, and living in the reality of the Resurrection are the things God specifically told us he wants us to know about the Last Days. They are things all Christians can and should unite on.

Unfortunately, in our Christian society today, there are lots of differing opinions about what else will happen in the future. Scholars tend to present their ideas on these things as "facts" or "doctrines," but we need to remember that prophecy is a complex study. Most of these are just theories about what will happen. Each theory then usually has 3 or 4 opposing theories. Theories are just guesses.

This is why there is so much debate in the Church and online about issues like the timing of the Rapture or the ethnic identity of the Antichrist. Wonderful, spirit-filled scholars have spent years studying and researching these things, but yet after all that study, many still disagree with each other – often angrily and bitterly.

Besides being a terrible witness, the disagreement of these scholars should tell us that these are very complex issues, not easily decided. And it should also tell us that if we place our faith in only one theory, it is possible we will prepare for the *wrong* viewpoint of the future! Given the eternal consequences of being wrong that Jesus laid out in the previous chapter, we need a form of preparation that is more assured.

KEY POINT: We need to stand on solid ground when it comes to getting ready for the Last Days.

I know what you are thinking, "I am sure my view of the Rapture, Antichrist, etc. is 100% correct. My Pastor and Denomination believe so too." Maybe they are correct - they base their opinions on the Bible after all. However, there are just as many pastors and denominations who believe differently, and who also base their opinions on the Word. If you are correct, they are mistaken. If they are correct, you are mistaken. I believe we need to hold our viewpoints on the Last Days more loosely than most do. We need to place our faith on doctrines not unproven theories - because we could be mistaken about a theory.

At Jesus' First Coming, nearly everyone was mistaken. The religious leaders were mistaken, the disciples were mistaken, and the regular citizens were mistaken. Nearly everyone was mistaken and misunderstood what the Old Testament prophecies were saying about Jesus. Isn't it possible that in the same way you and I, your church, and your denomination will be just as mistaken about what the New Testament is saying of His Second Coming?

So we need a **new paradigm** of how to get ready, a new way of thinking that doesn't reject the theories proposed by our churches and our denominations, but accepts other ideas as well – that the Last Days may happen in ways that will surprise us all. This is the humble approach, the meek approach. Wisdom is meek:

> *Who is wise and understanding among you?*
> *Let him show by good conduct that his works*
> *are done in the **meekness** of wisdom.*
> (Jam 3:13)

Unfortunately, the heated nature of the discussion of prophetic issues online makes a new paradigm in today's Christian culture very difficult. Many are so invested in being "right" about Last Days issues, they cannot see the danger if it turns out they've been mistaken. Emotions run so high on the two issues we mentioned that most Christians cannot see clearly enough to realize that a new paradigm is just a common-sense way to protect yourself, your family, and your church.

KEY POINT: The Last Days shouldn't be about being right or wrong, but about what we should *do* to prepare for them.

So, what would such a paradigm be? Perhaps we should divide our theories of the Last Days into two categories:

first, those things about which there should be no debate like the four rock sold beliefs we discussed earlier in this chapter, and second, those things about which there is serious debate and disagreement. And then we should treat these two categories *differently* in terms of how we prepare. Why is this important?

I'm sure you have heard the phrase, "Hope for the best, but prepare for the worst." This is good advice in most life situations. This phrase goes all the way back to 46 BC, when Cicero wrote to a friend saying, "You must hope for the best." And there is nothing wrong with hoping.

However, there is a lot wrong with not preparing for the worst. That is why we purchase insurance. We have spoken of hurricanes throughout this book as a symbol for the Last Days. The real-life Hurricane Florence took the roof off my house. Luckily, we had prepared for the worst and had bought insurance. And because of the insurance, we were able to fix our roof. Insurance is a great example of preparing for the worst. And in terms of preparing for the Last Days, I suggest you insure yourself as well. What do I mean by that? Can we buy a policy for that? No. But the principal is the same.

There are several rock-solid truths about the Last Days that all, or nearly all, Christians believe. We have already mentioned four of them. Jesus also said that there will be deception, war, famine, pestilence, earthquakes, an Antichrist, and there will be a Mark of the Beast. Of these things there is little to no disagreement. And just as importantly, He said He would rescue us prior to His Wrath:

*Wait for His Son from heaven, whom He
raised from the dead, even Jesus who delivers
us from the wrath to come.* (1 Thess 1:10)

Jesus is infallible. He is exactly whom we should trust. And we can take all these things to the bank. These things will happen. However, will Christians experience all these things during the Last Days before that rescue?

This is where it gets murky. Our interpretation of what He said about *when* His Wrath begins and *when* He will rescue believers is open to debate. Why else would so many scholars and teachers disagree about this? It is probably *the* major disagreement about the Last Days in our culture.

This ambiguity is why we need insurance. And it is where the idea of hoping for the best and preparing for the worst comes into play. We can and should hope for the best that the eye of the hurricane doesn't hit us, but we must "buy insurance" in case it does. We must prepare for the worst. Insurance is preparing for things EVEN IF WE HOPE WE WON'T EXPERIENCE THEM!

In the Spirit of humility, we should prepare our families and churches because perhaps our understanding of these issues is flawed in some ways, and we might experience deception, war, famine - and even the Antichrist. And given that the impact of being wrong about these things prior to the return of Jesus is so high – it's eternally dangerous if we're wrong - the smart and safe thing to do is prepare as if you're right AND prepare as if you're wrong! Prepare both ways. There is no downside to this type of preparation –

there is only upside – that you will truly be ready for Jesus no matter what the future holds.

This doesn't mean you change your view of prophetic events. But it does mean you prepare for more than just what you *think* will happen. You can both believe one viewpoint and still prepare for more than one possibility, just as in hurricane preparation.

> KEY POINT: All believers should prepare to both meet Jesus today, and at the same time, prepare to face the Antichrist.

I know this is a stunning statement to almost everyone reading this book. No matter what your personal opinion of the Last Days is, this statement has probably rocked your boat.

It means that those persons who favor a position that there is no Rapture or that the Rapture happens after the Tribulation should prepare spiritually as if they could meet Jesus any day. Because what if they've been wrong about their position? Imagine not being spiritually prepared to meet Jesus today! (Note: we all should be prepared to meet Jesus every day because of our own mortality, not just because of the Rapture.) Insurance is preparing for what you don't think will happen.

It also means that those persons who believe Jesus will rescue believers prior to the coming of Antichrist should also prepare to face that evil man just in case they're mistaken. Insurance means being prepared for what you don't think will happen.

And insurance also means that those persons who don't think they'll face the Last Days at all, let alone the Antichrist, should also prepare as if they will because maybe they'll be surprised!

This doesn't mean that any of these groups should change their opinions. They should continue to believe what they think the Bible says about these matters. It just means that all of them should *prepare* for both contingencies.

As we said, there is absolutely no downside to preparing for both sides of the argument. We cannot risk the lives and souls of others by stubbornly and pridefully refusing to prepare for all contingencies.

KEY POINT: This one, simple act of humility may save hundreds of millions of lives and souls because it is likely no one is completely correct in their Last Days views.

In the following chapters, we will begin to look at how a Christian can use this principle to prepare for each of the various the outer bands of the coming storm.

CHAPTER ELEVEN

Avoiding Deception

In the preceding chapters, we learned Satan's plan for the Last Days is a Strong Delusion designed to get people to eventually take the Mark of the Beast. This supernatural, unexpected deception will consist of a lie that is so attractive only those who love the truth will be able to overcome it.

The key role this deception plays in the Last Days is why, when the disciples came to Jesus asking about those days, the first thing Jesus' said was:

> Take heed that no one deceives you
> (Matt 24:4)

Jesus' primary concern for all who enter the Last Days is that they are not deceived. And it's God's Word that Satan is taking aim at in this deception just as he did in the Garden of Eden. Satan deceived Eve with a series of lies arranged to get her to doubt God's Word.

> Now the serpent was more cunning than any beast of the field which the Lord God had made. And he said to the woman, "Has God indeed said, 'You shall not eat of every tree of the garden'?" ... Then the serpent said to the woman, "You will not surely die. For God knows that in the day you eat of it your eyes

will be opened, and you will be like God,
knowing good and evil." (Gen 3:1-5)

Satan is still using the same strategy knowing that God's Word is the power of God. If he can get people to ignore God's Word, doubt God's Word, or believe it doesn't apply to them, then Satan can cause people to believe the Strong Delusion – "the Lie."

KEY POINT: God's Word is our protection against the delusion.

Satan has been hard at work for centuries getting people to ignore or reinterpret the Word. In the previous chapter, we described how one of the four things God specifically told us to not be ignorant of, God's plan for Israel, was reinterpreted by many churches. We also saw how many churches today are teaching that we need to "unhinge" ourselves from the Old Testament in direct opposition to another thing God told us not to be ignorant of. In this later case, these churches are ignoring 3/4 of the Bible!

But in the future, a greater deception is coming, one that will cause many of those sitting in our churches to "fall away" from true faith.

Let no one deceive you by any means; for that
*Day will not come unless the **falling away***
comes first (2 Thess 2:3)

Paul was not warning us about what will happen to those outside our church walls. Satan already has them in his power. This is about those who walk away or "fall away" from the Gospel. They are not truly saved, but they attend our churches and may even believe they are saved. But when the Lie comes, they will not love the truth and thus fall away.

In those days, will our current churches be able to protect churchgoers from "the Lie?" Probably not. At that time, our church buildings may resemble state-sanctioned churches in China. "The Lie" might be preached from the very pulpits we sit under today – by government order. The true gospel may have to go "underground." All pastors and small group leaders should be prepared for this contingency.

So the time to prepare and protect our churches is right now, using the prescription given by our Lord, Jesus. In the final week of His life, Jesus wanted to be sure the Church had His final instructions about what to do in the Last Days. So he gave us the Olivet Discourse (Matt 24 -25). These two chapters contain 13 separate commands designed to protect believers from the Strong Delusion.

Satan understands this, so he has been hard at work attempting to undermine Jesus' final commands about the Last Days. If the Deceiver can achieve that, he can leave churchgoers susceptible to the Lie. It is not surprising then that Matt 24 is one of the most hotly contested chapters in the Bible for a variety of reasons. But no matter what your opinion is on these "arguments," commands such as not being troubled by the Beginning of the Birth Pangs; preaching the Gospel, and enduring to the end of our lives are appropriate for all Christians – yet they are being ignored. So instead of arguing, we can concentrate on what is important – what Jesus told us to *do* in the last Days. Let's take a look at these commands one at a time because they are *eternally* important.

Take heed you are not deceived (Matt 24:4). As we stated at the beginning of this chapter. Deception is the hallmark of the Last Days. Jesus commands we "take heed" to avoid it. This Greek word, blepete, can mean to discern. We need discernment to avoid deception in this world. We need to be always on our guard to avoid it, sorting out what we see or hear in light of what God's Word says about these things.

Faith in Jesus is the only way to eternal life, and the Word of God is the only way to true wisdom. The Lie may promise biological or technological paths to these things. Obviously, this would sound very tempting, but if we stand on the Word, these things can be overcome.

See to it you are not troubled (Matt 24:5). When Jesus described the events in the Beginning of Birth Pangs, He used this phrase to show how we should react to them. When wars, rumors of war, famine, pestilences, and earthquakes happen, we are not to be troubled or terrified. And there is a very good reason; keeping a level head helps our evangelism. We discuss this more fully in the next chapter.

Endure till the end (Matt 24:13). Everyone should patiently endure till the end of their life and not give in to the Lie. In Chapter Eight, we explained this in depth, and how patient endurance was a trait that each and every single person who is kept from the hour of trial will exhibit.

(Preach) This Gospel of the Kingdom (Matt 24:14) Jesus told us that when the Gospel was preached to every people

group on Earth, then the end would come. What could be more important?

Learn this parable of the fig tree (Matt 24:32) We discussed this command at length in Chapter Four. Look what an enormous deception has happened because churches have not been learning this parable and uncovering the truth that we are the Final Generation.

Therefore, watch! (Matt 24:42) We discussed this other command in Chapter Five. Just as with the command to learn the parable of the Fig Tree, ignoring this command has led to an entire generation not realizing how close we are to the return of the Lord – and thus they aren't preparing.

The wise took oil in their vessels with their lamps (Matt 25:4) As we learned in Chapter Three, both the wise and foolish virgins light their lamps, but only the wise brought enough oil to keep them burning during the difficulty of the Last Days. We shouldn't imagine that it is "enough" to simply have said a sinner's prayer once in your life. We all must prepare and strengthen our faith.

Well done, good and faithful servant; you were faithful over a few things, I will make you ruler over many things. (Matt 25:21) As we also described in Chapter Nine, those who hide the great treasure that God gives us (the Gospel) will be cast into outer darkness. How many know this is God's expectation?

Who then is a faithful and wise servant, whom his master made ruler over his household, to give them food in due season? (Matt 24:45) God also expects us to act as Joseph in

121

the Last Days. In Chapter Thirteen we discuss how to do this in much more detail.

Inasmuch as you did it to one of the least of these My brethren, you did it to Me. (Matt 25:40) In Chapter Six we discussed this command and how it was being lived out by missionary Nathan Graves and his tiny church. This command exemplifies our basic marching orders in the Last Days – to love others and share the Gospel with them.

Those are ten amazing commands. Ten commands that most of the Church doesn't know. There are three more that involve the Great Tribulation. As we discussed in the last chapter, we are to hope for the best and prepare for the worst regarding that time period. As you look at these commands, you will see how we can put that advice into practice.

Let the reader understand the Abomination of Desolation (Matt 24:15) The greatest of Last Days deceptions will occur when the lawless one comes with Satanic power, false wonders, and miraculous signs as we saw in Chapter Seven. So being able to identify him is one of the most important preparations any church can make for Last Days.

The Apostle Paul gave us a sign to recognize the Antichrist and prevent us from being forever deceived:

> *The man of sin is revealed, the son of perdition, who opposes and exalts himself above all that is called God or that is worshiped,* **so that he sits as God in the temple of God, showing himself that he is God** (2 Thess 2:3-4)

The true Antichrist will take his seat in the Holy Place on the Temple Mount, probably in a newly built Temple of God. Only the real Antichrist will do this and this is a sign every Christian needs to know, even if they think they may not encounter him. What harm is there in knowing this sign?

What makes this tragic is that so many are only hoping for the best without preparing for the worst. It only costs a few hours to inform your family, small group, and church of these warnings. Again, what harm does it do? If you are correct and we don't face him, you only wasted a few minutes, but if you are wrong, not informing them could result in an eternity without Jesus.

And even if the Church is rescued first, the warning may not be wasted. Remember not everyone hearing our messages is saved! None of these commands of Jesus are a waste of time for us to teach. We must therefore prepare by arming those in our pews and those in our homes about the truth of God's Word. Whatever your eschatological beliefs, the Word is still true and worthy to be shared. Let's do it.

If they say to you, 'Look, He is in the desert!' do not go out; or 'Look, He is in the inner rooms!' do not believe it. (Matt 24:26) These commands fit into the same category: how believers can identify the false messiah and avoid his deception. Matt 24: 24-26 tells us the pretender to Jesus' throne will perform great signs and wonders – so great that they would fool even the elect if that were possible. The whole rest of the world will be deceived because they view events through the eyes of sight not the eyes of faith. They assume only God can perform miracles – they'll think this false Christ is Jesus.

But how can we be sure that this isn't Jesus? How will we know if it's a false Christ? We'll know because in this same scripture, Jesus gave us a sign to look for in order to know for certain whether or not it's Him - and that sign will be unmistakable.

Specifically, Jesus told us the whole world will see him in the clouds when He comes again. It will be like lightning from one end of the world to the other, bright, and loud, and every eye will see Him.

> For as the lightning comes from the east and
> flashes to the west, so also will the coming of
> the Son of Man be (Matt 24:27)

Any Jesus wannabe who doesn't come like that isn't the real Jesus. But how many churchgoers know this? This may be one of the most important prophecies in the Bible, but how many in your church know how to identify a false Christ, especially if he is performing incredible miracles? This false Christ may look like Jesus, talk like Jesus, perform great miracles like Jesus. But did he arrive like lightning in view of the entire world?

When you see the Abomination, those in Judea flee … Pray that it is not winter or sabbath. (Matt 24:16,20) Jesus was specific that when the Abomination of Desolation takes place, those in Judea should flee. This probably will include only a minuscule fraction of those reading this book. However, everyone can pray as Jesus commanded that the remnant of Israel flee at a time when it is not winter or a sabbath. Our prayers now will protect them at that time.

Those are Jesus' thirteen commands in the Olivet Discourse. And as you saw, they are discussed in almost every other chapter in this book. They are the heart of Last Days preparation. No wonder Satan is trying to prevent believers from knowing about them!

In our Christian culture, when we hear about deception, we usually think about "fake news" or something to do with politics. That is not the primary type of deception that Jesus warned us about. He was worried about the Deceiver causing us to ignore God's Word or to misinterpret it.

> *When anyone hears the word of the kingdom,*
> *and does not understand it, then the wicked*
> *one comes and snatches away what was*
> *sown in his heart.* (Matt 13:19)

Deception is only the first wave of several catastrophes to come. The second is war and chaos.

CHAPTER TWELVE

Overcoming War and Chaos

Nothing is more iconic of the Last Days than war and chaos. And nothing is more feared. As Jesus was explaining the Beginning of the Birth Pangs period to His disciples, immediately after warning them about the deception that was coming, Jesus warned them about war and chaos.

> *But when you hear of wars and commotions, do not be terrified; for these things must come to pass first, but the end will not come immediately* (Luke 21:9)

And Jesus's command to them - and to us by extension - was that we were not to be terrified by these things. The implication, of course, is that these events would terrify the average person. The threat of the use of nuclear weapons in the recent Ukraine Crisis is an example. All of a sudden, the Crisis went from a sterile conflict "over there" to one that might impact folks "over here." Instantly social media and traditional media sites lit up with discussions of how these things might affect you and me.

Thinking that wars and disturbances will only affect someone else is a major spiritual problem for believers in safe, Western culture. Many of us think what Nathan Graves and his church is doing in Albania is noble. But we don't expect to have to do it here. We have always considered our Western countries to be a safe space. And we like it like that.

However, that is changing. The fact that the pandemic, inflation, and the threat of nuclear war are worldwide problems is one of the reasons 9 out of 10 Pastors see them as the possible outer bands of a coming spiritual hurricane. The Bible teaches that most of the Birth Pangs are worldwide in scope.

In Revelation we learn that peace - or at least peace of mind - will be taken from the earth by events on a biblical scale!

> *Another horse, fiery red, went out. And it was granted to the one who sat on it to take peace from the earth, and that people should kill one another; and there was given to him a great sword.* (Rev 6:4)

Think about what this implies. It has been estimated that the world has only been without war for 268 scattered years throughout the entire time of man's existence.[6] So if war and chaos are the normal state of our world, this taking of peace does not imply the start of a new conflict. The world has always has had conflict. It has even had world wars; this must be something different.

It must be the taking of peace of mind from the inhabitants of the earth. That is what the Greek word translated peace in this passage means. What event or threat could remove this peace of mind?

The use of nuclear weapons is one. If nuclear weapons and fallout start to be spread, everyone would become anxious. So this taking away of peace of mind could be a sign of the

---

[6] http://www.ayww.org/faqs

use of these weapons. In Revelation, the red horse rider is also given is a great sword. He is given a weapon, a great weapon. Might this be a nuclear one?

A second possibility is some sort of worldwide ethnic or religious struggle affecting every corner of the globe. Imagine if every Muslim on the planet entered into jihad with his neighbors, or if some sort of inter- racial struggle began. That would also take peace of mind from the Earth.

And, of course, both the use of nuclear weapons and ethnic struggles could be happening simultaneously!

KEY POINT: *In the Last Days, peace of mind will be taken from the entire world.*

So all of us need to prepare ourselves for what is to come and what is already here. And for what we are going to do about these things as Christians, as followers of our Master. Our response is to be different than that of the world. We are to prepare the way for the return of our King in the hearts of those impacted by these things.

Jesus is the answer to a loss of peace; He is the Prince of Peace, after all. His perfect love casts out all fear. As we work to lift up the downtrodden, we must keep this in mind.

As wars and chaos continue to escalate, let's begin by understanding the types of conflicts about which Jesus warned us:

> *And you will hear of wars and rumors of wars*
> *... For nation will rise against nation, and*
> *kingdom against kingdom.* (Matt 24:6-7)

And as we saw at the beginning of the chapter, Luke adds an additional type of conflict: "commotions." The Greek word translated as "commotions" can be thought of as revolutions, riots, and chaos.

So Jesus tells us there are two basic types of conflict: war and riots. And they take place either on a nation against nation basis or on a kingdom against kingdom basis. Some of these will take place in our own neighborhoods, and some will take place in other parts of the globe. They'll also be "rumors of war" that we only hear about in the news.

In the English-speaking world, we read this passage and we think of nation rising against nation as being war between two countries. But the Greek word translated "nation" is ethnos which actually means ethnic group. Jesus told us ethnic groups will rise up against each other. So in addition to war on a nation-state level, the Last Days will be marked by ethnic struggle.

And isn't that what we are seeing in our world right now? News broadcasts feature struggles of black against white, rich against poor, young against old, Muslims against Jews, and Democrat against Republican. The governments and the media are attempting to separate us from each other on any and all bases. The days of peaceful protests like that of Martin Luther King, Jr. are over. I expect the intergroup conflicts to only escalate as further outer bands of the spiritual hurricane continue to hit us.

The other basis on which these wars take place is kingdom against kingdom. This implies that nations will form alliances, and the alliances will fight against each other. And this is exactly what we are seeing unfold in the Ukraine Crisis of 2022. In fact, the struggle appears to have started over this exact issue – preventing Ukraine from entering NATO. And as the conflict there dragged on, Russia came into alliance with Belarus, Iran, Syria, Iraq Brazil, India, South Africa and China. The outline of two great alliances seems to be taking shape: NATO and an alliance of totalitarian regimes. Will our world morph into a struggle of kingdom against kingdom? Yes. Jesus told us so directly. And it is a fearful thought because that is how world wars begin.

Jesus also describes the impact of these wars:

> *For nation will rise against nation, and kingdom against kingdom. And there will be famines, pestilences, and earthquakes in various places* (Matt 24:7)

Famine and disease are the natural consequence of conflict. Even when the shooting stops, the pain and hardship won't. In World War II, 19 to 28 million are thought to have died from disease and starvation.[7]

But how we are to react to these struggles is what the Christian must focus on:

> *But when you hear of wars and commotions, do not be terrified; for these things must come to pass first* (Luke 21:9)

---

[7]

https://en.wikipedia.org/wiki/World_War_II_casualties#:~:text=Deaths %20directly%20caused%20by%20the,deaths%20totaled%2050%E2%80 %9355%20million.

Jesus told us not to be terrified by any of these struggles. That when we see these horrible ethnic divides and chaos, we aren't to panic, which is the natural reaction. No, instead we are to remain calm.

Jesus explained that we are not to be terrified because these are the "things that must come to pass first." They are part of His plan. Nothing will happen that Jesus doesn't allow, and allow for his own purposes. So whatever happens to your country - or even if nuclear weapons are used - it must be something Jesus is allowing.

Remember that He is permitting catastrophes so that all who will be saved can be saved. We aren't to be terrified because we will be right where Jesus needs us to be – right next door to those who will be terrified.

People desire to live at peace almost more than anything. So, giving your neighbor the gift of peace – the Prince of Peace who dispels fear – is one of our primary goals in the Last Days. If we are at peace within ourselves, it will attract a frightened world.

KEY POINT: *His perfect love will cast out all fear.*

We should also remember Nathan Graves and how his little church handled the crisis of refugees flooding into their country, how they showed the love of Jesus to those displaced by the conflict, and how the Holy Spirit used their outreach to save many. We need to emulate this effort. If Pastor Graves was terrified by what was happening, this great harvest might not have happened.

These ever-intensifying conflicts will also give us another wonderful opportunity to live out the gospel in a way that is totally unexpected.

The unsaved expect Christians to serve those displaced by violence - it's pretty much what they assume Christians are called to do. But there is one thing that no unsaved person ever expects: that we would love and care for our enemies as Jesus commands - even those who have harmed us greatly. This is the very opposite of human nature.

KEY POINT: *In time of great discord and division, loving our enemies is a shock to those observing.*

We will likely see unspeakable things done to those we love, or even experience those things ourselves. If you are of one race, no one expects you to love and forgive those of another race who might have just beaten you. If you're "straight," no one expects you to love and forgive those who identify as LGBTQ who may have just had you thrown in prison. And if you are old, no one expects you to love and forgive a younger generation who may have taken away your health care. But it is exactly those sorts of things that Jesus expects from us in the Last Days. Forgiving and loving those who hate us may be the greatest form of evangelism of all. In these Last Days, in the midst of all the ethnic and racial division, every Christian will have the opportunity to love and forgive their enemies.

> *But I say to you, love your enemies, bless those who curse you, do good to those who hate you, and pray for those who spitefully use you and persecute you* (Matt 5:44)

It is not surprising that Jesus warned us that during the Last Days that the love of most will grow cold. But what did he mean? Will it be the love of most Christians growing cold? I actually think so. But it must not be you or I. We must remember that those we view as enemies - those who are creating the chaos - are not the enemy at all. They are actually the victims of our true enemy; they are currently held in bondage by the evil one. A bondage from which Jesus desires us to help free them.

God's master plan is to allow catastrophe which will include ethnic struggle and war. Our place amid those events is to be ambassadors of the Kingdom that is coming, to reach out to the hurting by showing them the love of Jesus, even those that consider themselves to be our enemies.

Finally, one of the great internal conflicts we will face as Christians will be how to juggle our allegiance to the country where we reside and our allegiance to the heavenly Kingdom. We must remember that we have dual citizenships.

> For our citizenship is in heaven, from which
> we also eagerly wait for the Savior, the Lord
> Jesus Christ (Phil 3:20)

Our first allegiance is to the Kingdom of Heaven and King Jesus not to our earthly Kingdom.

As the protests we currently see in our nations evolve into armed conflict and civil war, Christians will have to decide whether to take up arms to protect their local and national governments, or to work solely for the Kingdom of God. Which approach Christians take will depend on their view of the Last Days. Those like me, who believe we are already in those days understand that Western nations will likely fall in the near future anyway. We will spend our time preparing the way of the King rather than trying to hold on to a lifestyle that we've become accustomed to. This may be a decision all of us need to face in the near foreseeable future.

Until that time comes, I encourage everyone to pray for discernment so you will know what to do. As other waves of catastrophe overtake the planet, will we try to hold on to the life we have or let it go and follow Jesus? That may be the most difficult question we are required to answer.

CHAPTER THIRTEEN

Economic Collapse

When Bob Brown and I wrote the first edition of this book in 2018, a lot of people smiled and shook their heads when we suggested that one of the outer bands of the coming spiritual hurricane will be economic collapse. At that time the world economy, and especially the US economy, were the strongest they might have ever been. However, now just four years later, those knowing smiles have deepened into frowns. The Pandemic, supply chain issues, and runaway inflation are crippling world economies. Of course, according to what the Bible predicts, we *ain't seen nothin' yet*. In the USA, price inflation stands at about 10%, but in the Book of Revelation, it will end up at about 10,000%, we call that hyperinflation:

> *And I heard a voice in the midst of the four living creatures saying, 'A quart of wheat for a denarius, and three quarts of barley for a denarius; and do not harm the oil and the wine.'* (Rev 6:6)

In this passage, a voice is heard from the area of the Throne of God (it probably is God's voice) setting a price for grain. It is easy to read right past this passage because the term denarius is so unusual. In the Roman world of the First Century, a denarius was a coin that represented a day's wages. In my nation of the USA, the average daily wage in 2021 was $152.

The term "denarius" is interesting in several ways. First it reminds me of the "basic universal income" that the World Economic Forum is suggesting in something known as the Great Reset. Perhaps you have heard of it? We will discuss the Great Reset later in this chapter, but suffice it to say that a basic universal income is a daily wage that all people will receive in a sort of one-world, socialistic state. This basic income sounds suspiciously like the concept of a denarius in the First Century. Is this prophecy in Revelation confirmation that the Great Reset or something like it is going to happen? Perhaps.

Figure 5: Comparison of Denarius and Digital Currency

In the future what will this day's wages buy? We're told: a quart of wheat, which is enough to bake a single loaf of bread. At that point, in today's US dollars, the buying power will have so eroded that a person will work all day and be able to buy only a single loaf of bread with his/her $152. That is 10,000% hyperinflation.

There are countries where we're seeing that kind of hyperinflation already. In the African nation of Zimbabwe, a loaf of bread costs a million of their dollars. People often bring a wheelbarrow full of money to the market since its worth so little.

Even developed countries have experienced hyperinflation. After World War I, the nation of Germany was saddled with war reparation payments, a punishment for losing the war. When they missed a payment in 1922, France sent its troops into Germany's industrial region to confiscate manufactured goods as a make-good on the missed payment. Germany responded by closing the factories (rather than pay France), and printed money to pay its laid off workers.

This flood of extra money led to inflation, which led to more money being printed, the more prices rose, even more money was printed. Prices ran completely out of control. For example, a loaf of bread, which cost 250 marks in January 1923, had risen to 200,000 marks in November 1923. Sounds familiar, doesn't it? So the current inflation crisis in our world today is similar to what happened in Germany almost exactly 100 years ago.

KEY POINT: *According to the Bible, money is about to become almost worthless.*

If you noticed, war and the payment of war reparations led to the hyperinflation in Germany. War has this effect. So the catastrophe of war that we just examined in the last chapter will likely wreak havoc on the earth causing the means of economic development to be greatly curtailed. At that point, economic collapse is inevitable. So it's no surprise that Jesus warned an economic disaster will follow the war and chaos. And as we have seen with every other form of catastrophe in the end times, God will use these economic stressors to bring the lost to himself.

The Gospels simply state that there will be famines (Matt 24:7); not that there might be, but that there will be. Knowing this in advance, that there will be famines and food shortages in the Last Days, what should a Christian response be? Obviously, a caring Christian would put away food now to be used later during these famines. As we discussed in Chapter Eight, Jesus suggested exactly this solution when he taught his disciples the Parable of the Head of the Household.

In that parable, the wise and faithful servant feeds God's household at the "appointed time." What is the appointed time? It is the time God has chosen. In this case, it is most likely the appointed time of the end when the famines take place - the same famines Jesus prophesied would occur. In that previous chapter, we showed how this parable contains a riddle whose solution is "Joseph." Christian leaders need to emulate Joseph, the son of Jacob, who put away 7 years of food to provide for the famine that would follow.

The grain that Joseph set aside was used during the famine to feed both the Egyptians and Joseph's family: his brothers, father, nieces, and nephews. Jesus is telling us by means of this riddle how He wants his servants to act during the Last Days. He wants all of us, especially our leaders, to act like Joseph. Once we realize we are the Final Generation, this responsibility to be able to feed both our churches and the unbelievers will fall on us during the catastrophe Jesus said is coming. This is the same idea as Nathan Graves' outreach to the Syrian Refuges, but it may be in your neighborhood.

I have been putting food away since 2015 to provide for this purpose and have filled a storage unit, but our churches have the ability to put away much, much more. How much food should Christians be setting aside? The account of Joseph in the Book of Genesis actually tells us:

> Let Pharaoh do this, and let him appoint officers over the land, to collect one-fifth of the produce of the land of Egypt in the seven plentiful years. (Gen 41:34)

For seven years, Joseph had the Egyptians put away 20% of the food they produced. The biblical estimate then for how much each person in a church is to put away is 20% of their grocery bill.

After praying for God's provision, you can estimate that if you spend $400 a month on food, you should spend an additional $80 on reserves for the famine. For many people, this is the equivalent of giving up their Starbucks habit. In cases where this is too much of a hardship, cutting back on the amount of the original grocery bill consumed works also, still buying $400 but only eating $320 worth. Those in western democracies tend to buy more expensive food and more of it than is needed. Or perhaps a person could cut back in other areas of the budget. Remember that once prices rise to hyperinflation levels it is TOO LATE to put food away.

No matter what the price of wheat is, a quart of wheat is still a quart of wheat. Stored food and other items necessary for survival will be even more valuable in the future than they are today. They are immune to inflation.

But how long will our stored food provide for us once the famine begins? Isn't this just a pipedream that we will be able to provide for our churches and the unsaved God sends us? Well first, having something beats having nothing. And second, no, I don't think it's unrealistic because we are serving a God for whom all things are possible. Let's consider the feeding of the five thousand.

Jesus fed a multitude that day, and I think he will in the Last Days as well. In the prophetic letter to the Church of Pergamum in the Book of Revelation, Jesus tells us He will provide some of the "hidden manna." So I have every confidence that if we run out of food, God can provide and likely will.

But let's look at the account of the feeding of five thousand in more detail. Jesus fed the multitude, but he did it after a great act of faith. The faithful one was only a boy who remembered to pack his lunch. And although he was as hungry as everybody else that day, he gave all he had to the Lord. It was those very loaves and fish that Jesus multiplied.

In the Last Days, if we give all that we have put away, will Jesus multiply our gift? That is my opinion of what God's heavenly economy is like, however, God decides issues like that. We can only have faith that He will.

KEY POINT: *God is faithful. He will likely provide for those who give it all away.*

This is how we prepare for the catastrophe of famine and economic collapse of the end times, not by only putting away supplies for our own family and friends, but in anticipation of giving it away.

Now some will say God will provide anyway, why bother putting food away? He may, but isn't that presuming upon Him without taking action of our own to "pack a lunch?" And then again, He may not provide for those who refuse to step out in faith. God's ways are not our ways.

Water is also a likely need in the Last Days, and this is much simpler to provide. My family has dug a well in our yard and also have portable filtration "straws" for water if we're forced from our homes. All of these are small acts of faith. Jesus said there will be famines and we should take him at his word.

Now let us discuss the Great Reset. This term describes a resetting of the world economic system by the nations of the world and the United Nations. The World Economic Forum is the think tank spearheading this effort. Their plans are to acquire all the assets of every person on earth, and in return, to forgive all personal and national debt and give them a basic universal income. Basically, it's a socialist take-over of the world.

At one time, this was considered a conspiracy theory, but the World Economic Forum, comprised of billionaires and world leaders from nearly every nation, are now very up-front about this scheme. Although entire books can be

143

written about this topic alone, it should be obvious to everyone studying this reset that it appears the world economy and everything you own will be turned upside down in the next few years. Now is the time to prepare – there won't be opportunity later.

And as we saw, God will use the economic collapse, but so will Satan. He will use it and every other wave of catastrophe to position and eventually propel his man, the Antichrist, into a position of power.

First, he will use deception. Next, he will use war. The wars and chaos will deplete the nations of their economic strength. The economic collapse and famines that follow might be the final blow that allows the Antichrist to take power. He will literally tip the scales in his own favor by trading food for worship. The infamous Mark of the Beast will be just such a food for worship scheme.

You might be thinking, we'll be "outta here" by then, and yes, we might be. But there still are reasons we should put food away. The first is that the Last Days are a spiritual hurricane that begins with outer bands hitting before the main storm. It is likely we'll need food long before the Mark. Second, as we learned in Chapter Nine, we need to prepare for the worst - as if there is no Rapture. And finally, even if we are "outta here," someone else will need the food! As we mentioned earlier, in the letter to the Church of Pergamum, Jesus promised to provide "hidden manna." Might this be food put away by an earlier group of Christians that a latter group of Christians find? Absolutely. The Holy Spirit might lead them to it. The food we put away is for others after all, not ourselves, whether we share it with them or they find it after we're gone.

And as we've discussed, preparing for the worst means also knowing how to face this test and be able to recognize the Mark of the Beast. In 2021, there was a great deal of discussion whether the vaccines and their associated mandates were the Mark of the Beast. Although they had perhaps one of the six distinguishing features of the Mark, they obviously weren't the Mark. So any good manual on preparation for the Last Days must include these six features of the Mark found in Rev 13:16-18:

- The Beast, himself, must be present,
- The False Prophet initiates the Mark, so he's present,
- The Mark is always associated with worship of the Beast,
- The Mark is a physical sign on the forehead or hand,
- The Mark is always associated with either the name or number (666) of the Beast,
- It restricts buying and selling.

If all six features aren't present, what you are considering isn't the Mark. It's that simple.

The next question is just as important, if not more important: how can you avoid any such food for worship scheme, whether it is the Mark of the Beast or some precursor – ones that we may encounter soon? The answer is given in Revelation:

> *Then a third angel followed them, saying with*
> *a loud voice, "If anyone worships the beast*
> *and his image, and receives his mark on his*

145

*forehead or on his hand, he himself shall also
drink of the wine of the wrath of God, which
is poured out full strength into the cup of His
indignation. He shall be tormented with fire
and brimstone in the presence of the holy
angels and in the presence of the Lamb ...
Here is the **patience** of the saints; here are
those who **keep the commandments of God**
and the **faith** of Jesus.* (Rev 14:9-12)

Three things protect a believer from such tests: patience (which the Bible also translates as "patient endurance"), keeping the commandments, and faith. We have already seen in Chapter Seven how someone keeps the commandments of God, it is by loving Jesus and being empowered by the Holy Spirit.

The epistle of James describes how one acquires patient endurance:

*My brethren, count it all joy when you fall
into various trials, knowing that the testing of
your faith produces patience.* (James 1:2-3)

Patient endurance is developed over time by enduring other trials. So what you are going through right now is producing endurance for the future.

Paul describes how to produce faith or trust in God:

*So then faith comes by hearing, and hearing
by the word of God* (Rom 10:17)

It is acquired through study of God's Word, specifically through group study where we hear his Word spoken.

All these things take time. Nothing is instantaneous. These are practices that one acquires over a lifetime. God is slowly and faithfully preparing believers for what is coming. And the ever increasingly difficult outer bands of the spiritual hurricane that is hitting our world are strengthening the faith and endurance of the true believers. "Count it all joy when you fall into various trials." God is using them for our good.

After economic collapse, a scapegoat will need to be found for all the world's problems. When Nero lit the city of Rome on fire in AD 64, he needed a scapegoat, and he blamed the Christians. It is certain that Christians will be objects of persecution again. But God will use this persecution for His Glory as He has used every other catastrophe.

CHAPTER FOURTEEN

For the Sake of the Kingdom

In this book, we have seen how God is using various forms of catastrophe: war, disease, and economic collapse to reach the unsaved. Could God also use the persecution of His faithful believers to save the lost as well? The answer is a surprising - yes! Most of our readers have grown up in Western cultures, and for us it's hard to imagine that God could use our personal suffering. Yet God permitted his own son to die for our sins on a Roman cross and suffer unspeakable agony. That is how he expressed his mercy and love. It was that loving sacrifice that saved us.

Not only did Jesus lay down His life, but all the Apostles except one were martyred. Peter was even said to have been crucified upside down. The entire history of the church is littered with the bodies of those who died for Christ. If you've never read *Fox's Book of Martyrs*, it's a hefty volume outlining many of the early martyrs. It has been said that the blood of the martyrs was the seed of the church, and this type of persecution is already happening. The outer bands of the spiritual storm are hitting.

In the year, 2018, 215 million Christians experienced severe levels of persecution. In 2022, that number increased to 312 million - that is 1/7 of all Christians worldwide – the highest percentage in history.[8]

---

[8] https://www.opendoorsusa.org/christian-persecution/

And it is probably going to get a lot worse rather quickly. In the preceding chapter we discussed a Great Reset that billionaires and nations are planning - a socialist takeover of the world economic system and governments. However this will likely be much more than just economic.

When totalitarian governments assume power, they purge those who disagree with them. In last one-hundred years, governments like Soviet Russia, China, and Nazi Germany killed over 160 million dissenters. The Bible tells us another world-wide government is coming that will be *"drunk on the blood of the saints"* (Rev 17:6). "Oh, that must be the Beast Empire," you are thinking. No, this is the empire (Mystery Babylon) that precedes the Antichrist! So two purges of unprecedented proportions are coming; one of them prior to the rise of the Antichrist.

Surprising? I think we should be surprised if we don't suffer. Peter put it this way, he said:

> *Beloved, do not think it strange concerning the fiery trial which is to try you, as though some strange thing happened to you; but rejoice to the extent that you partake of Christ's sufferings, that when His glory is revealed, you may also be glad with exceeding joy* (1 Pet 4:12-13)

This is from the man that was crucified upside down. And Jesus himself had quite a bit to say about the persecution of his Saints as well. He expects us to take up our own crosses. He is sending us out as sheep among wolves. He says we will end up in court and be beaten, and he advises us against trying to save and protect our own lives if it means denying Him. So, we shouldn't be in the least bit surprised that God may use extreme persecution for His own purposes in the future as He has in the past. But how might God use this persecution for His purposes? How might persecution build the Kingdom? Let's see.

Jesus said blessed are the persecuted for righteousness' sake. He didn't say the persecuted were just okay; He said they were blessed and gifted to be persecuted. And Jesus didn't stop there. In the very next two verses, He takes this idea up a notch. He says we are to rejoice when others revile us or persecute us. This is the same idea Peter had. Jesus says this is the same way they persecuted His beloved prophets who went before us.

Now although this seems absurd from an earthly point of view, Jesus obviously meant what he said. And we should believe Him.

In the next couple verses in Matthew 5, Jesus that we are to be the salt of the earth and the light of the world. You can see how these two things might directly lead to persecution. Those desiring the decay of society hate salt. Those who love darkness hate the light. So if given the chance, these individuals and the spiritual powers behind them, will persecute those bringing restoration and light.

So, if we are being persecuted, those who are against our Lord are recognizing his Spirit in us and persecuting us for it. And for that we should rejoice greatly! It is the evidence that we are doing His will, which is much more important than temporary pain from persecution. Jesus continued in Matthew. He said:

> *A city that is set on a hill cannot be hidden.*
> *Nor do they light a lamp and put it under a*
> *basket, but on a lampstand, and it gives light*
> *to all who are in the house. Let your light so*
> *shine before men, that they may see your*
> *good works and glorify your Father in heaven*
> (Matt 5:14-16)

Christians are a city on a hill that is highly visible and cannot be hidden. Jesus' plan for his followers is to bring their deeds to the forefront, and those who persecute hate that the gospel is given that position. However, their persecution of the believer is also visible. This is a key factor, so let me state it again.

KEY POINT: *Because believers are a city on a hill, any persecution of those believers is highly visible as well.*

Jesus then delivers the punchline, He sums up this teaching, "Let your light so shine before men, that they may see your good works and glorify your Father in heaven." Good works give glory to God. Among the greatest of these good deeds is enduring persecution for righteousness' sake. And because believers are a city on a hill, those good deeds for which they are persecuted are highly visible – resulting in more praise – maybe in salvation for those watching it.

Humans may praise God for our deeds of service or for our love of others, but in a way, people have come to expect that from Christians. But when that good deed is refusing to deny Jesus or speaking the Gospel even when it is unpopular or illegal, those watching really pay attention. They recognize instantly that it is a work of God - that it isn't normal human nature - and that leads them to realize God must be real.

That is why it is said, "the blood of the martyrs is the seed of the church." This is a quote of the early church father, Tertullian. It was understood then, and it is understood now; the supernatural ability to endure persecution breaks down the resistance of the lost to the Gospel. Let's say it again:

> KEY POINT: *The supernatural ability to endure persecution breaks down the resistance of the lost to the Gospel.*

Just like all other catastrophes of the Last Days that we have discussed in this series, the purpose of persecution is to spread the Gospel. Hebrews 11:1 tells us faith is the evidence or proof of things not seen. Our acts of faith are the evidence to a fallen world that God is real. Enduring persecution is our ultimate act of evangelism.

How does the church return to that earlier understanding that God uses persecution as a form of witness? In fact, the Greek word martyr actually means "witness." I think people want to be able to reach this level of being sold out for Jesus, but aren't sure how. I am frequently asked how does someone prepare themselves or their families to face this type of persecution?

May I tell you a story to help explain it? Corrie ten Boom, the Dutch evangelist, once asked her father about preparing for persecution. Her dad asked her, "If you're going on a train ride, do I give you the ticket two weeks ahead of time?" "No," Cory said, "You give me the ticket right before the trip." "That's right," her father replied, "And it's the same with persecution. God will give you the strength to endure it right before you need it."

So you don't need to worry if you don't believe you have that strength right now. God will prepare Christians for persecution right before it happens. Each wave of catastrophe will be like a training exercise. As believers overcome each subsequent wave or outer band, they'll become more conformed to Jesus's image and less attached to the things of this world. The White Horse rider will take away truth. The Red Horse Rider will take away peace. The Black Horse Rider will take away possessions. So when the Pale, Green Horse Rider of persecution gallops up to us, we are ready.

Believers who have been prepared in this way, by the waves of catastrophe taking away their current way of life, may also be asked to deny Jesus and deny the Word of God. It is at this point they will be ready to stand up for God and affirm Jesus is Lord and God whatever the cost.

Corey Ten Boom and her family are most famous for hiding Jews in their home from the Nazis in World War II. The Jews escaped, but Corey, her sister, and father did not. They were sent to concentration camps and tortured. Only Corey survived the war.

A second aspect of persecution many may not have thought about is that we may be forced from our own hometowns. A very significant number of the Christians persecuted in 2021 were those forced from their homes. Just like Ukrainian

Christians fleeing the Russians, believers in the first century had to flee from Jerusalem. This scattered them throughout the surrounding nations. Did this surprise or disappoint God? Hardly. God used the scattering to spread the Gospel even further. I strongly suspect He will use persecution to scatter the Church in these Last Days as well.

Where your treasure is there your heart will be also. Where is the "X" on your treasure map? Is it the blessed hope? If you are valuing the things of this world, you won't be able to let them go. If you value the Kingdom of Heaven over this fallen world, you are ready for persecution. It isn't easy at all, but it is that simple.

God's Will is always best. It really all comes down to faith and trust in His Will. Do we trust God that the life to come is better than the physical one we have now? And that His rewards far outshine what we might surrender here.

CHAPTER FIFTEEN

Three Things to Do Today

The hardest part of any preparation is getting started. Amen to that! And I'm sure that as you've read this book, the amount of preparation material that the scriptures provide has probably seemed overwhelming. So in this final chapter of book, we are giving you three simple things you can do today (and every day) to begin to prepare for the Last Days. Even though we've discussed dozens of ways to prepare, what we're discussing in this final chapter may turn out to be the most impactful.

All human endeavors are pointless without prayer and the guiding of the Holy Spirit. Jesus said:

> I am the vine, you are the branches. He who abides in Me, and I in him, bears much fruit; for without Me you can do nothing. (John 15:5)

So, if you want to do things on your own, go ahead. But Jesus said you will accomplish nothing. Only abiding in Jesus produces fruit. Therefore, the very first thing that all of us should do is pray for guidance and empowerment. But where do we begin?

Believe it or not, the Bible tells us this as well, but it is a most unlikely source; it's the prayer known as the Lord's Prayer. It is probably the most famous prayer of all time, and if you're like me, you already have it memorized. If

157

you're going to utilize this prayer in preparation, you don't even have to memorize anything new!

The Lord's Prayer has six main petitions, or as some say intentions. And to some extent they mirror the coming waves of catastrophe. When we pray the Lord's Prayer, we can pray to prepare us for each wave. It's really a wonderful Last Days prayer.

The first thing to notice about this prayer is it's a prayer for the whole Church. "*Our* Father - give *us* this day - deliver *us*." The intentions are all plural. We are praying for all of us, not just ourselves. And although it can be prayed in its original form, it is also what is known as a topical prayer. In other words, every one of the six petitions is a memory aid to help remind us to pray additional requests for that topic.

The petition "*Our Father who art in heaven hallowed be thy name*" reminds us to praise God and to pray for the hollowing of his name. "Thy kingdom come" reminds us to pray for the topic of his kingdom etc. I think using the prayer in this way is most useful for Last Days preparation. Let's look at each petition and see how they apply.

The first petition, "*Our Father who art in heaven hallowed be thy Name*" is contrasted with the first wave of catastrophe: Satan's deceptions, which have the opposite effect of praising the Name of the Lord. I use this portion of the prayer to pray for the Church; that it avoids the deceptions of the evil one, his false prophets and false Christs. I pray the Church has discernment to know who these false agents of Satan are. I also praise God in this section as Creator, Savior, and intimate Father. After praying all those things, the Spirit often brings more special intentions to my mind, and I pray those as well. Then I move on to the second petition.

"Thy kingdom come" is contrasted with the second wave of wars, rumors of war, and chaos. As earthly kingdoms rise against each other, this petition reminds us that they will all pass away. However, Jesus's Kingdom will come, rule the whole earth, and never pass away. I earnestly pray that that Kingdom comes quickly. I also pray that the church is not terrified by what we see or will see, and to remember that these catastrophes are "the things that must take place." Which, of course, means that Jesus is in complete control. I also pray that Jesus's kingdom expands upon the earth, and for the salvation of many.

"Thy will be done on earth as it is in heaven" - it is at this point in the prayer that I pray that the Lord of the harvest send workers into his field. When Jesus sent His workers out two-by-two, this was his first instruction to them: to pray for more workers. So I pray that they will lead many to Christ, and that His righteousness fills the earth. I also pray that his workers trust in the Father's Will even when it's difficult.

This is also the point in the prayer where I choose to get quiet. I go silent. Just as Samuel said to the Lord, "Lord speak - your servant is listening." I listen for God's voice - for His Will which may be a new revelation, an instruction, or maybe an encouragement.

"Give us this day our daily bread" - in this section I pray for provision for all of God's people. This petition parallels the

coming economic collapse we spoke of in Chapter Thirteen. Daily provision will be much needed at that time. Currently I pray for provision and willpower for God's people to begin to stockpile food and other supplies for that appointed time right now.

"*Forgive us our debts as we forgive our debtors*" - loving our enemies and forgiving them for the horrible things being done and that will be done is perhaps the most challenging thing that is coming. This matches the catastrophe of persecution that is coming.

"*Lead us not into temptation, but deliver us from the evil one*" - the Greek word translated "temptation" is better thought of as a trial or testing than temptation. It's the same Greek word used in Revelation 3:10 where God promises to keep the Church of Philadelphia from the hour of *trial*. In this section of the prayer, I pray none of us receive more than we can handle, and that God's Spirit empowers and strengthens us every step of the way.

"*For thine is the kingdom and the power and the glory forever*" - this final petition reminds me to pray that all of us keep our eyes on the prize, not the events around us. That we remember that Jesus is coming soon, and we will be made like him. If we keep our eyes on Jesus, we can endure anything.

Saying a daily prayer for the Last Days is something we can and should do today and every day from now on.

If these Last Days prayers are the first thing we can do today, the second thing is to immerse ourselves in the Word of God - especially those sections related to prophecy – the

Torah, the Prophets, the Gospels, Thessalonians, Peter and Revelation. It's nice to see what Bible experts have to say, but nothing replaces hearing from God's voice directly.

A big problem that I encountered early in my Christian walk was studying the Word in terms of a verse here or there rather than in context. They say a verse out of context is a pretext. Many experts like to present verses in this way because it's easier to quote a verse than a whole book, but unfortunately, it's also easier to make a single verse say what you want it to say.

A number of the epistles can be read in a single sitting. A lot of times if I'm going to study a short passage, I will start by reading the entire book in which it's found, then go back and study the passage that I'm interested in. When I do this, I'm constantly surprised how the authors of Scripture frequently refer back to something they said a chapter or two earlier. This is something I would miss reading only a passage rather than multiple chapters.

The other thing that happens when you study a passage in its full context is you see how to apply the Scripture. The prophetic passage is usually found in the midst of other passages about how to live. These applicational passages are frequently ignored by the overwhelming majority of prophetic ministries who focus on what is going to happen and when it's going to happen, but avoid what to do about it. And the application or "what to do" is what really matters most. We are to be doers of the Word.

Last Days prayer and Last Days Bible study are the first two things we can do today, the final thing we can do is to join forces with a partner in your ministry. Our Lord sent out his disciples two-by-two. And in Luke 10, Jesus's first instruction to these disciples was to pray to the Lord of the harvest to send other workers into the field. The first of these workers to pray God provides is a like-minded brother or sister, or another family to come alongside you and your family. Pray for someone to help you apply all these preparation steps.

There are good reasons our Lord sent the disciples out two-by-two and not individually. Two persons form a valid biblical witness as we see in Deuteronomy 19:15. And where two or more are gathered in his name, there Jesus is as well. Two persons can encourage each other and hold each other accountable, spurring each other on to love and good deeds. And we are to do it all the more as we see the Day of the Lord approaching. This will be required in the Last Days when Christian life is going to get tough. We'll need each other.

A final reason is to maximize the spiritual gifts we've been given. It is likely that the team will have different gifts from the individual, and combining these gifts makes a more powerful team. Now some may think their spouse should be their sole partner in this endeavor, but that isn't what Jesus did. Although some of the disciples He sent out two-by-two were married, Jesus still sent them out with another disciple as well. I assume some were sent out two families at a time, not two persons at a time, and that is what I recommend for all of us who are married.

So there you have it - three things to add to your daily walk: prayer based on the Lord's Prayer, being immersed in Scripture, and a partner to walk through the ministry with daily. These three things will help you and encourage you for the task God has called you to.

Personally, my final thought for you as you embark into the Last Days is one of attitude. So many today view the Last Days as a fearful time of punishment. This is a mistake. As we've seen, although these days will be difficult, they are essentially a good thing. They are God's great effort to reach the lost whom he loves so much. So much so, that he sent His only Son to humble himself and die on a cross for them.

And as we saw in Chapter Eight, they are also a time when God will refine His Bride and transform us into the people that God desires.

So Jesus excitedly calls us to follow Him into the great unknown of the Last Days, to leave our nets behind - which are symbolic of our attraction and love of this world - and to join Him as servants and friends. And together to daily work with Him to reconcile the lost to the God who loves them.

We invite you to join His "road crew." May the Lord bless you in this endeavor.

Perhaps I will see you on the "road."